CLUB LAW MANUAL

SECOND EDITION

CLUB LAW MANUAL

SECOND EDITION

Kerry Barker and Henry Stevens

WS
&H

Wildy, Simmonds & Hill Publishing

Club Law Manual, 2nd edition

British Library Cataloguing in Publication Data
A catalogue record for this book is available from the British Library

ISBN 978-0854900-62-6

Typeset in Baskerville MT Pro and Optima LT by Cornubia Press Ltd
Printed and bound in the United Kingdom by CPI Antony Rowe, Chippenham, Wiltshire

First published in 2011 by
Wildy, Simmonds & Hill Publishing
58 Carey Street
London WC2A 2JF
England

FSC
www.fsc.org
MIX
Paper from
responsible sources
FSC® C013604

Contents

PART SIX – LIABILITIES

Appendices **175**

Table of Cases

Table of Statutes

Table of Statutory Instruments

Table of Guidance, Codes of Practice, etc

References are to page numbers

Table of European Materials

Preface

It was with both pleasure and trepidation that we accepted the commission to revise and update Ken Pain's 'Club Law Manual'. Ken is an old friend and his work had become a standard for those involved in the business of members' clubs, whether they were simply interested members or officials such as club secretaries, treasurers and chairs. It was also to be found on the bookshelves of local authority licensing officers, police officers and civilian staff working in licensing departments, and many high street solicitors.

As requested we have brought the work up to date (as of the autumn of 2010) but we have also tried to build upon the original work by adding chapters on gambling and fund-raising. We have omitted the important explanations of the transitional provisions of the Licensing Act 2003, which were very necessary when this version of the manual was first published because they are no longer in play. We have retained, however, Ken's informative use of analogies with the law as it was under the provisions of the Licensing Act 1964.

Perhaps more important we have tried hard to follow Ken's lead in making the manual both approachable and readable for the interested club member or official and their legal advisers. The manual is not a textbook full of legal footnotes but is intended to make the law relating to members' clubs understandable and to give pointers as to when the need for expert legal advice arises. Whether we have succeeded is for others to judge.

At the time of writing the new coalition government announced the transfer of responsibility for licensing places selling or supplying alcohol from the Department for Culture, Media and Sport (back) to the Home Office. It is anticipated, therefore, that in due course references to the Secretary of State for the DCMS and that department's website will be replaced by references to the Home Secretary and the website of the Home Office.

Kerry Barker
Henry Stevens
Guildhall Chambers, Bristol
October 2010

Preface to First Edition

Over the years many people have pointed out that it is difficult to find a simple guide to the law as it affects members' clubs. There are, of course, several works that contain information relevant to members' clubs and the way they operate, but for club managers and their advisers to find the relevant parts is not always easy. This has encouraged me to write this manual on club law. The advent of the Licensing Act 2003 has presented me with the ideal opportunity.

The book concentrates on members' clubs and the numerous laws that affect how they are managed, the statutory authorities that have an interest in them, and the relationships between officers, members and the clubs themselves. The guidance is not limited to the provisions of the Licensing Act 2003. Other important legislation, dealing with employment, food hygiene, health and safety and public liability are also covered. General advice in relation to the proper conduct of meetings and formulating club rules is also offered.

The opening chapters of the book focus on the Licensing Act 2003 and the controls it introduces in relation to the supply of alcohol and the provision of many types of entertainment. There are few references to case law because much of the existing case law will no longer be relevant once the new Act is in full force. Many of the provisions of the Licensing Act 2003 will, I have no doubt, be interpreted by the High Court in due course but, for the time being, the words of the statute are the best guide we have.

I hope this book will be useful to practitioners, to all those concerned in running clubs, to the police and the statutory authorities, and not least to the new licensing committees of the local authorities. I hope it is sufficiently readable to be of assistance to those who have taken on the running and management of members' clubs.

The book does not answer every question that may arise in relation to members' clubs. Complex or unusual problems are beyond the scope of the book, but I am confident that most aspects of club management are touched upon, and that where the text does not give a comprehensive answer, enough information is given to enable the reader to find other, more detailed, advice fairly easily. My aim has been to present the information in a way that will enable busy people to find what they are looking for quickly.

Inevitably, in a work that features entirely new law, some of the views expressed are my own. As case law develops, some of those views may prove to be incorrect, but I believe they are soundly based on experience.

Since the provisions of the Licensing Act 2003 on transitional applications came into effect on 7 February 2005, Chapters 1 and 3 are of most importance to readers coming to grips with the new licensing regime. I recommend that these two chapters be studied with some urgency. Other aspects of the new law can then be examined at a more leisurely pace.

Although the text of the book is based on the Act of 2003, it is important to remember that until the second appointed day (still to be designated as this book goes to press), when the Act will come into full force, new applications for club registration certificates are still to be made to the magistrates following the procedures in section 41 of, and Schedule 5 to, the Licensing Act 1964. Since those procedures will become obsolete soon, they are not covered in this work.

Kenneth W Pain
March 2005

1 Introduction

1.1 The nature of clubs

There are primarily two types of club, the proprietary club in which the club's assets are owned by an individual or a company, for example, and a members' club in which the assets are owned by the members.

Examples of members' clubs include sporting clubs, working men's clubs and political clubs. They are not-for-profit organisations run for the benefit of the members or for charitable purposes chosen by the members. By contrast, proprietary clubs such as nightclubs and leisure clubs are run as businesses with the purpose of making a profit for their owners.

This book provides guidance for those concerned with members' clubs.

1.2 Members' clubs

A members' club consists of an association of like-minded people who come together to establish premises that can be used by them to further the interests they share.

Often, a members' club is described as a club that is run by its members for the benefit of its members in general. Apart from those who may be employed by the club, no individual derives financial benefit from the activities of the club. All assets belong to the members generally, and all profits accrue for the benefit of the members or for any charity that the club may choose to support. It is these features, relating to the management of a club, that distinguish a members' club from a proprietary club. If a members' club is dissolved, its assets should be distributed among those who are members at the moment of dissolution, in equal shares, unless the constitution demands that they be passed on to a particular charity or to some other organisation with similar objectives.

Similarly, the members jointly own any alcohol purchased by the club. So when alcohol is served to a member it does not constitute a sale to him because he owns it already. Instead, what takes place is a supply and the member pays for it only to maintain equality between the members.

1.3   Legal status

The majority of clubs and associations are run as unincorporated associations. They are simply formed by way of a constitution or agreement between the members for whatever purpose the association of those people is required. That purpose may be sporting or political or to do with the local community, for example. This is the simplest form of club structure and the easiest to run and operate. However, as far as the law is concerned that unincorporated association does not have any legal status beyond that of a collection of members. It does not have its own legal personality.

An unincorporated association cannot own property, cannot employ people and cannot take or defend a legal action. Associations get around these problems by making provision in the rules for a member or members, usually the officers of the association, to act on their behalf to sign contracts, for example. Since unincorporated associations cannot own property, some members will be appointed as trustees to hold property on trust for all the members. The rules will often seek to limit the liabilities of those individual members by providing for indemnities from the membership as a whole. A consequence of unincorporation is that on the rare occasion that something goes seriously wrong all the members of the association are liable.

Alternative solutions are to convert the association into a limited company, to register as a mutual society or to register as a charity.

1.4   Limited companies

Forming or converting the association or club to a limited company enables the club to become a legal entity in its own right, separate from the individual members. There are two types of company for these purposes, one with an issued share capital where ownership and control lies with the shareholders (not normally appropriate for members' clubs) and a company limited by guarantee where each member guarantees to pay a nominal sum in the event of the company being unable to meet its obligations.

There are several advantages to incorporation. As a distinct legal entity the club is able to enter into contractual arrangements and own property, and save for the liability of individual members in cases of fraud or negligence, for example, individual members can only be held responsible for the club's debts and contractual obligations to the value of their guarantee. However, the registration and administration of limited companies is more onerous and there are legal penalties for failure to comply. All companies require various legal instruments such as a Memorandum and Articles of Association which must be registered with Companies House. The annual accounts must be presented in a prescribed form to Companies House where they will be open for public inspection. The incorporated club will be subject to the provisions of company law and must have directors. Some members may be prohibited from being directors because of their previous involvement with other companies or their financial status.

Clubs or associations should consider forming a limited company if they own assets of value, such as property and equipment, they engage in selling significant volumes of goods to non-members or they organise major events where liability to risk is an important consideration.

1.5   Mutual societies

Registration as a mutual society is often not considered. The relevant legislation, the Industrial and Provident Societies Act 1965 and the Friendly Society Acts of 1974 and 1992 and their predecessors aimed to regulate such organisations as co-operatives, mutual societies, credit unions, early building societies, housing associations and working men's clubs. In many respects registration as a mutual society is ideally suited for larger membership clubs. Mutual societies are overseen by the Financial Services Authority, which must approve all rule changes and receive a copy of the annual accounts. In most instances the structure, management and governance of the club remain unchanged by converting to mutual status. Mutual status confers limited liability on the members and establishes the club as a legal entity in its own right capable of entering into contracts as a corporate body. In many instances this is a cheaper and more flexible route than incorporation as a limited company.

1.6   Registered charity

It is now possible for members' clubs to apply for registration as a charity. There are two main benefits. Charitable registration establishes the club as a corporate body and legal entity. Charities are also able to benefit from more favourable tax treatment including Gift Aid on donations, discretionary relief on rates and other tax benefits.

To meet the charitable registration requirements the club must fulfil two criteria. First, it must provide one of several charitable purposes. These now include 'the advancement of public participation in sport' and 'the provision of recreational facilities or the organisation of recreational facilities, with the object of improving the condition of life for the person for whom the facilities or activities are primarily intended'. Second, the club must demonstrate that it provides a 'public benefit'. Guidance on these aspects is available from the Charity Commission.

Charitable registration requires the club and its officers to comply at all times with the charity regulations, including the annual provision of a trustees report and accounts, and to be open for inspection by the regulator at all times. The most important part of the regulator's function is to ensure public confidence and trust in all charitable activities. De-registration as a charity is a difficult process and so application for registration should not be undertaken without careful consideration. An alternative for sports clubs is to apply for registration with the Community Amateur Sports Club Scheme.

Community Amateur Sports Clubs can apply to be registered with Her Majesty's Revenue and Customs (HMRC) to claim tax relief. There are very considerable and important tax advantages. The club has to demonstrate that it is open to the whole community without discrimination, it is organised on an amateur basis, and that it provides facilities for and promotes participation in an eligible sport. Again, more information is available on the HMRC website at www.hmrc.gov.uk.

1.7   Licensing of members' clubs

Successive governments have recognised the difference between members' clubs and proprietary clubs and the value to communities provided by members' clubs. When introducing the Licensing Bill to the House of Lords, Baroness Blackstone said:

> We recognise the value to the community of registered members clubs such as working men's or political clubs. We recognise that such clubs are private premises to which access is restricted and where alcohol is not supplied for profit. We intend to protect the special position of such clubs. Although they will have to promote the licensing objectives in the same way as other licensed premises, they will not require the full premises licence. The Bill will, however, bring clubs into line with other premises in relation to sales to and consumption by children. (*Hansard*, HL Deb, vol 641, col 645, 26 November 2002)

Members' clubs have the following advantages under the LA 2003 when compared with licensed premises:

- there is no requirement for the club to have a designated premises supervisor to be responsible for the sale or supply of alcohol;

- there is no need for a member of the club or an employee to hold a personal licence;

- the provision of late night refreshments to members and their guests is not regulated;

- the police do not have powers to order immediate closure;

- when a court orders the closure of premises in a defined area that order will not apply to members' clubs;

- the police and officers of the licensing authority have fewer rights of entry.

In some areas members' clubs have come under strong pressure from police licensing officers and licensing authority officers to apply for a premises licence as opposed to a club premises certificate. Such pressures should be resisted if the club is to retain these advantages. The powers of the police and local authority to control the activities of the club are much greater if the club has a premises licence.

1.8   The licensing system

All premises in which licensable activities (see Chapter 2) are undertaken have to be licensed. The licensing authority is the local authority for the area in which the premises are situated.

The form of 'licence' required for a members' club is known as a 'club premises certificate'. In order to be eligible for the grant of such a certificate the club must comply with qualifying conditions designed to maintain the distinction between a members' club and a business.

Licensing Act 2003, s 4 sets out four aims or objectives. Each licensing authority must carry out its functions under the Licensing Act 2003 'with a view to promoting the licensing objectives'. They are:

- the prevention of crime and disorder;

- public safety;

- the prevention of public nuisance; and

- the protection of children from harm.

Licensing authorities have to publish policy statements and, when making decisions, must have regard to those published policies.

The Secretary of State has issued published guidance to licensing authorities. The latest issue was published by the Home Office in October 2010. Licensing authorities must also have regard to that guidance.

1.9   Club Law Manual – the aims of the book

The purpose of this book is to provide advice and guidance to those associated or dealing with members' clubs either as officers, committee members, ordinary members, staff, regulatory authorities (local councils), the police or legal advisers.

It is, however, a manual and as such is not intended to deal comprehensively with areas that demand textbooks in their own right such as employment law, health and safety law or food safety law.

The manual is divided into six parts:

Part One – Licensing: dealing with club premises certificates and the relevant law under the Licensing Act 2003 relating to the supply of alcohol, the provision of refreshments and entertainment.

Part Two – Gambling: the relevant parts of the Gambling Act 2005.

Part Three – Fundraising: the impact of relevant legislation on the ability of members' clubs to raise funds for the general benefit of members or chosen charitable purposes.

Part Four – Hearings and Appeals: hearings before local authority licensing committees and appeals to the magistrates' court under both the Licensing Act 2003 and the Gambling Act 2005.

Part Five – Internal Regulation: club rules and procedures, management of clubs, staffing and responsibility for the conduct of members and guests.

Part Six – Liabilities: the liability of clubs, their members and officers to fellow members and guests and others for things done or actions taken by or on behalf of the club.

PART ONE

LICENSING

2 Licensable Activities

2.1 Introduction

Only if a members' club undertakes what are referred to in the Licensing Act 2003 (LA 2003) as 'licensable activities' will it need any sort of statutory authority to operate as a club.

2.2 Licensable activities

'Licensable activities' are defined in the LA 2003 (s 1(1)) as:

(a) the sale by retail of alcohol,

(b) the supply of alcohol, by or on behalf of a club, to or to the order of a member of the club,

(c) the provision of regulated entertainments, and

(d) the provision of late night refreshments.

Since most members' clubs wish to be able, at the very least, to supply intoxicating liquor to members and guests, most need authority in the form of a club premises certificate.

2.3 Qualifying club activities

In relation to members' clubs the following activities are also defined by the LA 2003 (s 1(2)) as 'qualifying club activities':

(a) the supply of alcohol by or on behalf of a club to, or to the order of, a member of the club,

(b) the sale by retail of alcohol by or on behalf of the club to a guest of a member of the club for consumption on the premises where the sale takes place, and

(c) the provision of regulated entertainment where that provision is by or on behalf of a club for members of the club or members of the club and their guests.

2.4   Sale and supply of alcohol

Alcohol is defined in the LA 2003 as meaning spirits, wine, beer, cider or any other fermented, distilled or spirituous liquor, but does not include:

(1)   alcohol which is of a strength not exceeding 0.5% at the time of sale or supply;

(2)   perfume;

(3)   flavouring essences;

(4)   Angostura Bitters;

(5)   alcohol included in a medicinal product;

(6)   denatured alcohol;

(7)   methyl alcohol;

(8)   naphtha; or

(9)   alcohol contained in liqueur confectionery.

The 'sale by retail' of alcohol is a sale to any person other than off sales made to:

(1)   a trader for the purposes of his trade;

(2)   a club which holds a club premises certificate for the purposes of that club;

(3)   the holder of a personal licence for the purposes of making sales authorised by a premises licence;

(4)   the holder of a premises licence for the purpose of making sales authorised by that licence; or

(5)   the premises user in relation to a temporary event notice for the purpose of making sales authorised by that notice.

The 'supply of alcohol to members or guests' means in the case of a members' club the supply of alcohol by or on behalf of a club to, or to the order of, a member of the club, or the sale by retail of alcohol by or on behalf of the club to a guest of a member of the club for consumption on the premises where the sale takes place (LA 2003, s 70).

2.5   Regulated entertainment

'Regulated entertainment' is defined in LA 2003, Sch 1.

Schedule 1, Pt 3 contains the relevant definitions:

(1)   a performance of a play – being the performance of any dramatic piece whether involving improvisation or not which is given wholly or in part by one or more persons actually present and performing and which, whether by speech, singing or action, involves the playing of a role. 'Performance' includes a rehearsal;

(2)   an exhibition of a film – meaning any exhibition of moving pictures;

(3)   an indoor sporting event – which is a sporting event which takes place wholly inside a building and at which the spectators present are also wholly inside that building. 'Building' means a roofed structure (other than a roof which can be opened and closed) and includes vessels and moveable structures. 'Sporting event' means any contest, exhibition or display of any sport. 'Sport' includes any game in which physical skill is the predominant factor and any form of physical recreation which is also engaged in for the purposes of competition or display;

(4)   a boxing or wrestling entertainment – which is any contest, exhibition or display of boxing or wrestling;

(5)   a performance of live music;

(6)   any playing of recorded music – 'music' includes vocal or instrumental music or any combination of the two;

(7)   a performance of dance;

(8)   entertainment of a similar character to the performance of live music, the playing of recorded music or the performance of dance if it takes place in the presence of an audience and is provided (at least in part) for the purpose of entertaining that audience.

In addition, the provision of entertainment facilities, defined as 'facilities for enabling persons to take part in entertainment which involves making music, dancing or similar activity for the purpose of or for purposes which involve the purpose of being entertained' are deemed to be within the provision of regulated entertainment. So, for example, the provision of a dance floor for the use of members and their guests amounts to the provision of entertainment facilities as distinct from the 'performance of dance' which would be entertainment provided by professional dancers.

Also, in circumstances where a club premises certificate did not include the performance of live music and the playing of recorded music, the provision of karaoke facilities would constitute the provision of entertainment facilities.

2.6   Exemptions from 'regulated entertainment'

Schedule 1, Pt 2 contains exemptions from the definition of regulated entertainment.

The showing of films the main purpose of which is to demonstrate a product, advertise goods or services or provide information, education or instruction does not constitute the provision of regulated entertainment.

Incidental music, live or recorded, is not regulated entertainment provided it is incidental to an activity which itself does not comprise regulated entertainment.

Live broadcasts provided via the media of television and radio are not regulated under the LA 2003.

Religious services are exempt as is music which accompanies Morris dancing!

2.7   Late night refreshments

Late night refreshment is deemed to be the provision of hot food or drink between the hours of 11pm and 5am. Members' clubs are exempt from the controls of the LA 2003 if the provision of hot food or drink is limited to the provision to a member of a recognised or 'qualifying' club or to a guest of such a member. Clubs which have the benefit of a club premises certificate are 'qualifying' clubs.

3   Club Premises Certificates

3.1   Introduction

As explained in Chapter 2, if a members' club wishes to carry out any of those licensable activities referred to as 'qualifying club activities' then it needs the authority of a club premises certificate. In order to obtain such a certificate from the local authority (the 'licensing authority') the club must be appropriately 'qualified'.

3.2   Qualifying clubs

In order to qualify for a club premises certificate the club must satisfy five general conditions (LA 2003, s 62). They are:

(1)   under the rules of the club no one may be admitted to membership or admitted for any of the privileges of membership until 2 days have elapsed between their application and membership itself;

(2)   the club rules must prevent anyone who becomes a member without initial application or nomination from enjoying the privileges of membership until 2 days after their becoming a member;

(3)   the club must be established and conducted in good faith;

(4)   the club must have at least 25 members;

(5)   alcohol can only be supplied on the premises to members by or on behalf of the club.

In addition, if the club wishes to supply alcohol there are three further qualifying conditions (LA 2003, s 64):

(6)   that the purchase and supply of alcohol on behalf of a club must be managed by an elected committee of adult club members;

(7)   that no one involved in the purchase of the alcohol should receive any commission at the expense of the club;

(8)   that nobody involved in the supply of alcohol should receive any monetary benefit from the supply of alcohol by the club to its members and guests.

These conditions are designed to ensure that the club's character is maintained, and that it does not become a public house. The supply of alcohol remains under the control of the members and does not pass into the hands of a single person or group of persons. If it did, the club would, in truth, have a proprietor and the club premises certificate would no longer be appropriate.

Should a club's membership fall below 25 then the club is allowed 3 months within which to recruit sufficient additional members to take it to or above that number. Otherwise the club premises certificate will be withdrawn by the licensing authority (LA 2003, s 90)

'Good faith' simply means a genuine commitment to the principles that qualify the club for its premises certificate. It is to be judged in accordance with a number of factors set out in the LA 2003, s 63. They are:

(1)   any arrangements restricting the club's freedom of purchase of alcohol;

(2)   any provision in the club's rules, or other arrangements under which money or property of the club and any gain arising from the club's activities is or may be applied for purposes other than for the benefit of the club as a whole or for charitable, benevolent or political purposes;

(3)   arrangements for giving members information about the finances of the club;

(4)   books of account and other records kept to ensure the accuracy of that information; and

(e)   the nature of the premises occupied by the club.

Those pre-conditions could cause problems for some old 'clubs' such as friendly societies, industrial and provident societies and miners' welfare institutes where, for example, traditionally, premises have been owned by an employer or another body. Special provision is made in the LA 2003 to ensure that such societies, registered under the Industrial and Provident Societies Act 1965 or the Friendly Societies Acts 1974 and 1992, and institutes fall within the qualifying conditions (LA 2003, ss 65 and 66).

3.3 Application for a new club premises certificate

A club may apply for a certificate for any premises that are occupied by, and habitually used for the purposes of, the club. An application for a club premises certificate must be submitted to the local authority for the area in which the premises are situated. LA 2003, Pt 4 deals with such applications, and with other matters relating to club premises certificates.

The form of application and certain other matters – the fees payable, notices to be given, and requirements concerning the advertisement of applications – are to be found in regulations made by the Secretary of State under powers granted by the Act. In particular the Licensing Act 2003 (Premises Licences and Club Premises Certificates) Regulations 2005 (SI 2005/42).

When the application is submitted, the club must make a declaration, in writing, that it is a qualifying club. The declaration must be sent to the licensing authority. It must be in the form prescribed in the regulations.

The forms can be downloaded from the Department for Culture, Media and Sport (DCMS) website at www.culture.gov.uk/what_we_do/ alcohol_and_entertainment/ 3189.aspx.

The application must include:

- an operating schedule;
- a plan of the premises;
- a copy of the club's rules;
- the appropriate fee;
- such other matters as may be prescribed in the regulations.

The regulations require that the application is advertised to enable 'interested parties', that is local residents and businesses and councillors, to make representations to the local authority, and that copies of the application are served on the 'responsible authorities'.

Responsible authorities include:

(1) the chief officer of police for the police area in which the premises are situated;

(2) the fire authority for any area in which the remises are situated;

(3) the enforcing authority for Health and Safety at Work etc Act 1974 purposes for the area;

(4) the local planning authority for the area;

(5)   the department of the local authority responsible for minimising or preventing the risk of pollution of the environment or harm to human health (usually the Environmental Services Department); and

(6)   the local weights and measures authority.

It is wise always to check with the licensing authority as to who are the 'responsible authorities' in its area and find out the addresses of those authorities for service.

3.4   The application form

The first part of the form calls for the following information:

• the name and address of the club;

• the name and address of the club secretary, or person performing the duties of a club secretary;

• confirmation that the premises are occupied and habitually used by the club;

• the date from which the applicant wishes the certificate to start, and, if it is to be valid for a limited time only, the date on which it is to end;

• a general description of the club;

• the number of persons likely to be on the premises at any one time, if more than 5,000.

In the next part of the form, the club's operating schedule is to be set out. It includes:

• the regulated entertainments, if any, which are to be provided by the club;

• the entertainment facilities, if any, which are to be provided by the club;

• whether or not the club will supply alcohol to, or to the order of, members; if so, whether the supply will be for consumption on or off the premises or both; standard and non-standard times for the supply; and any seasonal variations;

• the hours during which the club premises are to be open to members and guests, including any seasonal variations and non-standard hours (for more about licensing hours, see Chapter 4);

- any adult entertainment or services, activities or other matters that may give rise to concerns in respect of children (the examples of such matters given in the notes to the form are nudity or semi-nudity, films for restricted age groups and the presence of gambling machines but legal advice will be needed as to the law relating to sexual entertainment venues);

- the steps the club will take to promote the licensing objectives (often identified during a risk assessment).

The regulated entertainments which may be provided are:

- a performance of a play;

- an exhibition of a film;

- an indoor sporting event;

- a boxing or wrestling entertainment;

- a performance of live music;

- any playing of recorded music;

- a performance of dance;

- live music, recorded music or dance which takes place in the presence of an audience and is provided wholly or partly to entertain that audience.

The entertainment facilities which the club may wish to supply are:

- making music;

- dancing; and

- other similar entertainment.

A club which includes any of the above entertainments or entertainment facilities in its operating schedule must give further details, including whether or not the entertainment will take place indoors or outdoors, timings, and seasonal variations.

The fee payable on making the application for a certificate is on a scale depending on the non-domestic rateable value of the premises. The fee scale can be found on the DCMS website.

As mentioned above, the application must be accompanied by a plan of the relevant premises in the prescribed form, a copy of the club rules, and the declaration that the club is a qualifying club. The licensing authority may wish to refer to the rules to be satisfied that the club is a qualifying club and that its club operating schedule is not inconsistent with its rules. The requirement to submit a copy of the rules is not overridden by the requirement to submit a declaration as to the qualifying status of the club; both must accompany the application.

3.5   Plans

Plans must be drawn to the standard scale of 1:100, unless the relevant licensing authority has notified the applicant, in writing, that it will accept another scale. The plan must show:

- the extent of the boundary of the building, if relevant, and any external and internal walls, and, if different, the perimeter of the premises;

- the location of points of access to and egress from the premises;

- if different, the location of escape routes from the premises;

- where the premises are to be used for more than one qualifying activity, the area to be used for each;

- where the supply of alcohol for consumption on the premises is to take place, the location(s) on the premises where alcohol will be consumed;

- fixed structures, including furniture, or similar objects temporarily in a fixed location, which may affect the ability of individuals on the premises to use exits or escape routes without impediment;

- the location and height of any stage or raised area relative to the floor;

- where the premises include any steps, stairs, elevators or lifts, their location;

- where the premises include any room(s) containing public conveniences, the location of the room(s);

- the location and type of any fire safety and any other safety equipment including, if applicable, marine safety equipment; and

- the location of any kitchen(s).

Plans may include a legend that enables the symbols on them to be understood.

3.6   Advertisements

An applicant for a club premises certificate must advertise the application:

- by displaying a notice containing certain information (see below). The notice must be displayed prominently, at or on the premises to which the application relates, where it can conveniently be read from outside the premises. It must be of a size equal to or larger than A4, printed legibly in a font size equal to or larger than 16, on pale blue paper. Multiple copies of the notice must be displayed on premises covering an area of more than 50 metres square. The notice must be displayed for a continuous period of not less than 28 consecutive days, starting on the day following the day the application is given to the relevant licensing authority; and

- by publishing a notice in a local newspaper or, if there is none, in a local newsletter, circular or similar document circulating in the vicinity of the premises, again containing certain information (see below). The notice must be published on at least one occasion during the period of 10 working days starting on the day after the application to the licensing authority.

The wording of the requirement to publish a notice in the press is interesting. Earlier legislation required press advertisements to be placed in a newspaper circulating in the district. *R v Westminster Betting Licensing Committee, ex parte Peabody Donation Fund Governors* [1963] 2 QB 750 was authority for the view that the newspaper in question did not have to be a local paper, as long as it circulated in the relevant district. In the regulations the words used suggest that publication in a national newspaper will not do, even though it may circulate in the relevant area.

The information which must be included in both the notice displayed on the premises and in the newspaper advertisement is:

- the club qualifying activities which it is proposed to carry on from the premises;

- the name of the club;

- the postal address of the club premises, or if there is no postal address, a description of the premises sufficient to enable the location and extent of the premises to be identified;

- the postal address and, where applicable, the worldwide web address where the register of the relevant licensing authority is kept, and where and when the record of the application may be inspected;

- the date by which an interested party or responsible authority may make representations to the relevant licensing authority;

- a statement that representations should be made in writing; and

- a statement that it is an offence knowingly or recklessly to make a false statement in connection with an application, and the maximum fine to which a person is liable on summary conviction for the offence.

3.7   Determination of the application

Generally, when a licensing authority receives an application for a club premises certificate and the authority is satisfied that the applicant has complied with the application procedures described above, it must grant the application (*British Beer and Pub Association, Association of Licensed Multiple Retailers, British Institute of Innkeeping v Canterbury City Council* [2005] EWHC 1318 (Admin), [2005] LLR 353).

The obligation to grant is subject only to the proviso that the authority may impose upon the certificate any conditions that are considered to be consistent with the operating schedule submitted as part of the application.

The authority must also, if appropriate, impose a mandatory condition concerning the exhibition of films, irresponsible promotions of alcohol sales or supplies, direct dispense of alcohol into the mouth of the consumer, free tap water, age verification, and the availability of alcohol in the smaller prescribed measures.

If relevant representations are made, however, the authority must hold a hearing to consider them, unless the authority, the applicant and each person who has made representation agree that a hearing is unnecessary

Having had regard to the representations, the authority must then take such steps, if any, as it considers necessary for the promotion of the licensing objectives.

The steps that an authority may take for the promotion of licensing objectives are:

- to grant the certificate subject to modifications to the conditions attaching to it. Conditions are regarded as modified if any of them is altered or omitted, or any new condition is added;

- to include in the certificate a mandatory condition concerning the exhibition of films;

- to exclude from the scope of the certificate any qualifying club activities to which the application relates; or

- to reject the application.

The LA 2003 prohibits the inclusion, in a club premises certificate, of authority for off-sales unless there is also a provision for consumption on the premises; any conditions attached to the certificate must be consistent with this prohibition.

A licensing authority may grant a certificate subject to different conditions in respect of different parts of the club premises or in respect of different qualifying activities. Conditions may, therefore, be imposed in relation to a function room that do not apply to a members' bar and vice versa. Similarly, a condition may restrict the provision of late night entertainment though it is of no relevance to the supply of alcohol generally.

3.8   Guidance

In relation to members' clubs the Guidance issued by the Secretary of State includes:

STEPS NEEDED TO PROMOTE THE LICENSING
OBJECTIVES

6.13   Club operating schedules prepared by clubs, as with operating schedules for premises licences, must include the steps the club intends to take to promote the licensing objectives. These will be translated into conditions included in the certificate, unless the conditions have been modified by the licensing authority following consideration of relevant representations. Guidance on these conditions is given in Chapter 10 of this Guidance.

6.14   The Secretary of State wishes to emphasise that non-profit making clubs make an important and traditional contribution to the life of many communities in England and Wales and bring significant benefits. Their activities also take place on premises to which the public do not generally have access and they operate under codes of discipline applying to members and their guests.

6.15   Licensing authorities should bear these matters in mind when considering representations and should not attach conditions to certificates unless they can be demonstrated to be strictly necessary. The indirect costs of conditions will be borne by individual members of the club and cannot be recovered by passing on these costs to the general public.

Whilst in relation to conditions it states:

PROPOSED CONDITIONS

10.7   The conditions that are necessary for the promotion of the licensing objectives should emerge initially from ... a certificate holder's risk assessment which applicants and clubs should carry out before making their application for a ... club premises certificate. This would be translated into the steps recorded in the ... club operating schedule which must also set out the proposed hours of opening.

10.8   In order to minimise problems and the necessity for hearings, it would be sensible for ... clubs to consult with responsible authorities when schedules are being prepared. This would allow for proper liaison before representations prove necessary.

IMPOSED CONDITIONS

10.11 The licensing authority may not impose any conditions unless its discretion has been engaged following receipt of relevant representations and it has been satisfied at a hearing of the necessity to impose conditions. It may then only impose conditions that are necessary to promote one or more of the four licensing objectives. Such conditions must also be expressed in unequivocal and unambiguous terms to avoid legal dispute.

10.12 It is perfectly possible that in certain cases because the test is one of necessity, where there are other legislative provisions which are relevant and must be observed by the applicant, no additional conditions at all are needed to promote the licensing objectives.

For advice on the way in which licensing authorities should deal with hearings when relevant representations have been made in relation to an application for a club premises certificate, reference should be made to Chapter 9. Chapter 10 deals with appeals.

3.9   Specific conditions

3.9.1   Films

Where a club premises certificate authorises the exhibition of films, it must include a condition that the admission of children is to be restricted. Where the certificate specifies the British Board of Film Classification, the admission of children must be restricted in accordance with its recommendations, unless the licensing authority has given notice to the club that its own recommendations are to be applied. Where such a notice has been given, or where no classification body is specified in the certificate, the restrictions recommended by the licensing authority must be observed. For these purposes 'children' means persons under the age of 18.

3.9.2 Associate members and guests

If the rules of a club provide for the sale of alcohol on behalf of the club to associate members or their guests, no condition may be imposed upon the premises certificate that would have the effect of preventing such sales from taking place.

Similarly, if the rules of a club allow for the provision of regulated entertainment on club premises, by or on behalf of the club and for the benefit of associate members or their guests, no condition may be attached to the premises certificate that would negate that rule.

3.9.3 Plays

Generally, if a club premises certificate authorises the performance of plays on the premises, the licensing authority may not attach a condition which relates to the nature of the plays which may be performed or the manner in which they are performed. The authority is not, however, prevented from attaching any condition that it considers necessary on the grounds of public safety.

An example of when it may be appropriate for a licensing authority to attach a condition which would restrict the nature of plays or the manner in which they may be performed might be where the size of the stage or other equipment are such that the use of certain effects would cause danger.

3.9.4 Off-sales

The LA 2003 introduced the concept of a certificate that specifically authorised off-sales. A club premises certificate may not, however, authorise the supply of alcohol for consumption off the premises unless it also authorises the supply of alcohol to members for consumption on those premises.

In addition, any certificate that authorises supply for consumption off the premises must include the following conditions:

- such supply may be made only when the premises are open for the purpose of supplying members with alcohol for consumption on the premises;

- the alcohol supplied for consumption off the premises must be in sealed containers; and

- the supply in question must be made to a member of the club in person.

3.10   Mandatory conditions introduced in 2010

In 2010, by the Licensing Act 2003 (Mandatory Licensing Conditions) Order 2010 (SI 2010/860), the government imposed additional conditions on all premises licences and club premises certificates which authorised the sale or supply of alcohol for consumption on the premises. The new conditions imposed responsibilities on 'the responsible person' defined in the LA 2003 as 'any member or officer of the club present on the premises in a capacity which enables him to prevent the supply in question' (s 153(4)).

The conditions had to be added to all new certificates and were imposed retrospectively on all existing club premises certificates without the need for those certificates to be recalled and amended. In other words, they were deemed to be attached to all premises licences and club premises certificates.

The conditions are:

(1)   the responsible person shall take all reasonable steps to ensure that staff do not carry out, arrange or participate in any irresponsible promotions;

(2)   the responsible person shall ensure that no alcohol is dispensed directly by one person into mouth of another (other than where that other person is unable to drink without assistance by reason of a disability);

(3)   the responsible person shall ensure that free tap water is provided on request to customers where it is reasonably available;

(4)   ... the club premises certificate holder shall ensure that an age verification policy applies to the premises in relation to the sale or supply of alcohol. The policy must require individuals who appear to the responsible person to be under 18 years of age (or such older age as might be specified in the policy) to produce on request, before being served alcohol, identification bearing their photograph, date of birth and a holographic mark;

(5)   the responsible person shall ensure that where alcohol is sold or supplied (otherwise than in secure containers made up in advance) it is available in the following (small) measures:

(a)　beer or cider: ½ pint,

(b)　gin, rum, vodka or whisky: 25 ml or 35 ml, and

(c)　still wine in a glass: 125 ml,

and that customers are made aware of the availability of those measures.

Irresponsible promotions (ie sales or supplies of alcohol) are defined as:

(1)　games or other activities which require or encourage or are designed to require or encourage individuals to drink a quantity of alcohol within a time limit (other than to drink alcohol sold or supplied on the premises before the cessation of the period in which the responsible person is authorised to sell or supply alcohol), or to drink as much alcohol as possible;

(2)　provision of unlimited or unspecified quantities of alcohol free or for a fixed or discounted fee to the public or to a group defined by a particular characteristic (other than any promotion or discount available to an individual in respect of alcohol available for consumption at a table meal);

(3)　provision of free or discounted alcohol or any other thing as a prize to encourage or reward the purchase and consumption of alcohol over a period of 24 hours or less;

(4)　provision of free or discounted alcohol in relation to the viewing on the premises of a sporting event where that provision is dependent on the outcome of the race, competition or other event or process or the likelihood of anything occurring or not occurring;

(5)　selling or supplying alcohol in association with promotional posters or flyers on, or in the vicinity of, the premises which can reasonably be considered to condone, encourage or glamorise anti-social behaviour or to refer to the effects of drunkenness in a favourable manner.

3.11　The certificate

When a licensing authority grants an application for a club premises certificate, it must give notice of the grant, forthwith, to:

• the applicant;

• any person who made a relevant representation; and

• the chief officer of police for the area in which the premises are situated.

The authority must also issue the club with a premises certificate and a summary of it.

If relevant representations were made, the notification of grant must include the authority's reasons for its decision and any steps it has taken to promote the licensing objectives. The licensing authority must give notice to the same people of any decision to reject an application for a club premises certificate. Again, the notice given must state the authority's reasons for rejecting the application.

Club premises certificates and summaries of them must be in the form prescribed in regulations. In particular, a club premises certificate must:

- specify the name of the club and its relevant registered address;

- specify the address of the premises to which the certificate relates;

- include a plan of the club premises;

- specify the qualifying club activities for which the premises may be used; and

- specify any conditions to which the certificate is subject.

'Relevant registered address' is the address given by the holder of the certificate as the one to be recorded in the licensing authority's records.

3.12   Theft or loss of the certificate

LA 2003, s 79 deals with the theft or loss of a club premises certificate or summary. It provides that if a club premises certificate, or a summary of one, is stolen, lost, damaged or destroyed, the club may apply to the relevant licensing authority for a copy. The licensing authority may charge a fee for providing a copy.

When a licensing authority receives an application for a copy document, it must provide a copy if it is satisfied that the original has been lost, stolen, damaged or destroyed; and, in the case of theft or loss, that the club has reported the matter to the police. The copy provided must be certified to be a true copy by the authority. It must be a copy of the original document in the form in which it existed immediately before it was lost, stolen, damaged or destroyed. A certified copy of a certificate or summary has the same effect as the original document for the purposes of the legislation.

3.13   Duration of the certificate

Once granted, a club premises certificate has effect until such time as it is withdrawn by the licensing authority or lapses as a result of being surrendered by the club (LA 2003, s 80).

A certificate does not have effect during any period when it is suspended.

There is no requirement to apply for periodic renewal.

3.14   Changes of rules, names and addresses

From time to time a club may wish to change its name or its address, or make alterations to its rules. LA 2003, ss 82 and 83 concern such matters. A club is at liberty to make changes of this kind without having to apply to the licensing authority, but the club secretary must notify the licensing authority of any such changes. This duty applies to any club that holds a club premises certificate, or any club that has made an application for a certificate which has still to be determined by the authority.

The notice must be accompanied by the club premises certificate or, if that is not practicable, by a statement of the reasons why it cannot be produced and the appropriate fee.

When an authority receives a notice of change of name or of club rules, it must amend the premises certificate accordingly.

The obligation to amend does not, however, apply to any notification that would have the effect of changing the club premises. If a club wishes to change its premises it must apply to vary its premises certificate.

Club secretaries must give notice of any change of name or club rules within 28 days of the day on which the change is made. Failure to give the notice within the prescribed period is an offence for which the secretary could be fined a sum not exceeding £500.

It is curious that notice of these changes is to be given to the licensing authority only. There is no obligation to inform the chief officer of police, nor is the licensing authority under a duty to tell the police about any change that is made. Problems may well arise where the police are not aware of a change, particularly to club rules. To avoid such difficulties, it would be good practice to advise the police of any changes.

Should there be a change in the club's relevant registered address, notice of the change may be given to the relevant licensing authority so that it can change the record in its licensing register. If a club ceases to have authority to use an address that it has used as its relevant registered address, it must give notice of that fact to the licensing authority, as soon as reasonably practicable. The notice must include details of a new address that is to be the club's relevant registered address. A fee is payable on making such a notification.

The need to give notice of a change of registered address is likely to arise where there is a change of club officers. For example, if the registered address has been the address of the club secretary, and a different person is elected to that office, the club's authority to use the outgoing secretary's address may come to an end.

A notice of change of registered address must be accompanied by the club premises certificate or, if that is not practicable, a statement of the reasons for the failure to produce it. The licensing authority must amend the club premises certificate upon receipt of notice of a change of relevant registered address.

If a club fails to give notice of a change of registered address, the club secretary commits an offence that may be punished by a fine not exceeding £500.

3.15   Variation of the certificate

Occasionally, a club may wish to make alterations to its club premises. If so, it must apply for a variation of the club's premises certificate. The procedures for variation are set out in LA 2003, ss 84–86.

The application must be accompanied by the club premises certificate or, if that is not practicable, a statement of the reasons for failing to provide it.

The form of application is prescribed by regulations and can be downloaded from the DCMS website.

The form calls for, among other matters, a description of the change contemplated; details of the effect it would have on the club operating schedule; and details of any additional steps to be taken by the club to promote the licensing objectives. The fee payable on making the application is on a scale depending on the rateable value of the premises.

An application for the variation of a club premises certificate must be advertised, and notice given to the responsible authorities, in the same way as for an original application for a certificate (see para 3.6).

Generally, when a licensing authority receives an application for the variation of a club premises certificate and it is satisfied that the applicant has complied with all the requirements relating to advertisements, it must grant the application.

If, however, 'relevant representations' are made in respect of the application for variation, the authority must hold a hearing, unless the applicant and each person who has made such representation agree that it is not necessary to do so.

Where there is a hearing, the authority, having regard to the representations, must take such steps as it considers necessary for the promotion of the licensing objectives.

The steps that might be taken are:

* the modification of the conditions of the certificate, by altering or omitting any of them, or by adding any new condition; or

* the rejection of all or part of the application.

The licensing authority is not empowered to modify or add conditions that do not relate to the variation sought.

Whether granting an unopposed application, or making a determination following representation, the licensing authority must comply with its duties in relation to the mandatory conditions concerning the sale or supply of alcohol and in respect of the exhibition of films.

When a licensing authority grants an application for the variation of a club premises certificate, it must give notice of its decision, forthwith to:

* the applicant;

* any person who made a relevant representation; and

* the chief officer of police for the area in which the premises are situated.

If relevant representations were made, the notice of decision must include the reasons for reaching that decision and any steps taken to promote the licensing objectives. The notice must also specify when the variation is to take effect. The commencement date will be either the date specified in the application for variation or, if that date is before the date on which the applicant is notified of the decision, a later date specified by the licensing authority in the notification.

If an application, or any part of it, is rejected, the authority must also give notice of the decision to the persons listed above. Again, the notice must be given forthwith and it must specify the reasons for the rejection.

The procedure described here may not be used to effect any substantial change to the premises to which the certificate relates. Consequently, if a club wishes to move to completely different premises, an application will have to be made for a new premises certificate.

3.16 Minor variations

In 2009 in recognition of the overcomplicated processes involved in making applications for what were comparatively minor variations of club premises certificates and premises licences, the government introduced revised procedures for minor variations through the Licensing Act 2003 (Premises Licences and Club Premises Certificates) (Miscellaneous Amendments) Regulations 2009 (SI 2009/1809).

The amendments prescribed the forms, advertising requirements, fees and content of the licensing authority's register in relation to minor variations. The purpose was to make applications for variations less costly and less time consuming where the variations proposed would not have an adverse effect upon the promotion of any of the licensing objectives.

The new forms for making an application for a minor variation are available on the DCMS website and from licensing authorities. The advertising requirements are limited to placing a white A4-size notice at the premises for a period of 10 working days following the day on which the application was given to the licensing authority.

There is no requirement to serve copies of the application on the responsible authorities. It is up to the licensing authority to consult those authorities, as it considers appropriate. It is always good practice, however, to keep the police and fire authorities aware of any proposed application for a minor variation.

Any application for a minor variation must be accompanied by the set fee.

Applications for minor variations cannot be made so as to:

(1)   vary substantially the premises to which it relates;

(2)   add the supply of alcohol to members or guests as an activity authorised by the certificate; or

(3)   authorise the supply of alcohol to members or guests at any time between 11 pm and 7 am or increase the amount of time on any day during which alcohol may be supplied to members or guests.

The licensing authority must consult such responsible authorities as it deems appropriate and take into account any representations they make or any received from interested parties within 11 working days from the day when the application was received.

If the licensing authority considers that the variation(s) proposed could not have an adverse effect on the licensing objectives then it must grant the application. Otherwise it must reject it. The licensing authority's decision must be made within 15 working days starting on the working day after the application was received. If a decision is not made within that 15-day period the application is deemed rejected and the fee must be returned. There is, however, provision for the licensing authority to treat the original application as a new application by agreement with the applicant thus setting a new timetable.

3.17 Review of the certificate

Interested parties, responsible authorities or members of a club may apply to the licensing authority for the review of a club premises certificate (LA 2003, ss 87–89).

For example, local residents may seek a review of a certificate if they contend that a change in the way the club is run – by introducing more powerful sound reproduction equipment, say – undermines the licensing objective of preventing public nuisance.

The form of application is prescribed by the Licensing Act 2003 (Premises Licences and Club Premises Certificates) Regulations 2005 and can be downloaded from the DCMS website.

The form calls for a statement of the grounds for review, which must be based on at least one of the licensing objectives, and for information in support of the application.

The same regulations require that the person making the application must give notice of the application to the club, and to each responsible authority. The notice must be accompanied by a copy of any attachments submitted with the application; and the notice must be given on the same day as the application is given to the licensing authority.

There is no requirement for the applicant for a review to advertise the application to the public; the authority must do this.

The licensing authority may reject a ground of review specified in a notice of application if it is satisfied that:

- it is not relevant to one or more of the licensing objectives; or
- if made by an interested party or a club member, it is frivolous, vexatious or a repetition.

A ground for review is repetitious for these purposes if it is:

- identical or substantially similar to a ground for review specified in a previous application in respect of the same club premises certificate, or to representations considered by the authority before it determined the application for the grant of the certificate; and

- there has not been a reasonable interval of time since that earlier application for review or the grant of the certificate.

If the authority rejects a ground for review of a certificate, it must notify the applicant of the decision. In addition, if the ground was rejected because it was frivolous or vexatious, the notice of rejection must give the authority's reasons for that decision.

The authority must give notice of rejection even where only a part of the grounds for review has been rejected. In such circumstances, the notice must make clear that a part of the grounds has been rejected and set out the reasons for the partial rejection.

When a licensing authority receives an application for the review of a club premises certificate from a person or body who has complied with the prescribed application procedures, and it has itself complied with specified time limits for the receipt of relevant representations, it must arrange a hearing.

For details of the procedure at hearings, see Chapter 9.

At the hearing, the authority must consider the application and any relevant representations that it has received. Having had due regard to those representations, the authority must take such steps as it considers necessary for the promotion of the licensing objectives. Such steps may include:

- the modification of any condition attached to the certificate, by altering or omitting a condition or by adding a new one;
- the exclusion of any qualifying club activity from the scope of the certificate;
- the suspension of the certificate for a period not exceeding 3 months;
- the withdrawal of the certificate; or
- leaving the certificate in its existing state (LA 2003, s 88(3)(4) and (6)).

The authority must keep in mind the requirement to include in certificates the mandatory conditions concerning the supply of alcohol for consumption off the premises and the exhibition of films.

When determining an application, the authority may order that any modification made, or any exclusion of a qualifying activity, is to have effect for a specified period only. That period may not exceed 3 months.

The licensing authority must give notice of any determination of an application for review and the reasons for the decision reached to:

- the club;

- the applicant;

- any person who made a relevant representation; and

- the chief officer of police for the area in which the premises are situated.

The authority's determination does not have effect until the period allowed for any appeal to be lodged against the decision has elapsed or, where notice of appeal is given, until that appeal is dealt with.

Where a local authority is both a relevant licensing authority and a responsible authority, it may apply for the review of a club premises certificate in its capacity as a responsible authority; and, in its capacity as a licensing authority, it may determine the application (LA 2003, s 89).

3.18   Surrender of the certificate

If a club decides that it wishes to surrender its club premises certificate it may give notice to that effect to the licensing authority. The notice must be accompanied by the club premises certificate or, if that is not practicable, by a statement of the reasons for the failure to produce it. The certificate lapses when the authority receives the notice (LA 2003, s 81).

3.19   Withdrawal of the certificate

As noted above, a club premises certificate generally has effect until such time as it is either surrendered by the club or withdrawn by the licensing authority.

Where the licensing authority has reason to believe that a club no longer qualifies for a premises certificate in relation to a qualifying activity included in the premises certificate, it must give notice to the club of withdrawal of the certificate, so far as it relates to that activity (LA 2003, s 90).

The club has a right of appeal against the withdrawal.

If the failure to satisfy qualifying conditions consists solely of the fact that there are fewer than 25 members, the notice of withdrawal must state that it does not take effect until the end of a period of 3 months following the date of the notice, and that it will not take effect at all if, by the end of that period, the number of members has risen to at least the minimum qualifying number (25).

Nothing in the Act prevents a licensing authority from giving a further notice of withdrawal, at any time, if it has reason to believe that the club no longer satisfies a qualifying condition.

A certificate may also be withdrawn by the licensing authority as a consequence of a review hearing.

4 Purchase and Supply of Intoxicating Liquor

4.1 Introduction

As mentioned in Chapter 1, whilst members' clubs are treated differently from licensed premises, in passing the LA 2003 the government was anxious to bring them into line as far as the sale or supply of alcohol to children and young persons is concerned. Differences remain, however, in relation to other aspects relating to sale and supply.

LA 2003, Pt 7 contains many, but not all, of the offences created by the Act. Different penalties are allotted to different offences sometimes by reference to the standard scale of financial penalties (fines) available in a magistrates' court and at other times the maximum penalty is given in the section creating the offence. There remain some 'licensing' or alcohol-related offences that are without the Act.

4.2 Licensing hours

The previous concepts of 'permitted hours' and 'drinking-up time' were abolished by the LA 2003. Licensing authorities can control the opening hours of clubs by attaching conditions to the club premises certificate but can do so only with a view to promoting the licensing objectives and decisions have to be made on a case-by-case basis.

The application form requires the applicant to stipulate opening hours for the premises and the hours between which each of the chosen licensable activities will be provided. If no relevant representation is received by the licensing authority in relation to such matters, then the club premises certificate must be granted in accordance with the application.

If relevant representations have been received, then the licensing authority can, if justified, attach conditions limiting both the opening times for the club and the hours during which the club can be open, in effect imposing a time limit for the consumption of alcohol on the premises. This was held to be the consequence of requiring the opening hours of the premises to be included in the operating schedule in the case of *R (Daniel Thwaites Plc) v Wirral Borough Magistrates' Court* [2008] EWHC 838 (Admin), [2008] LLR 536.

4.3   Children and young persons

Prior to the implementation of the LA 2003, it was a matter for each members' club as to the age at which children and young people were either allowed on the premises or allowed to consume alcohol. Members' clubs were expected to act as good parents. The only legal restriction was that alcohol could not be given to a child under the age of 5 except in an emergency or upon medical advice.

Members' clubs are now treated in the same way as other licensed premises in relation to the protection of children from harm through the sale or supply of alcohol.

The expression 'child' is used in the LA 2003, but means different things in different sections. So, for example, there is a prohibition on the presence of children in areas used exclusively or primarily for the sale of alcohol. In those cases a child is deemed to be a person under the age of 16 years. Whereas it is an offence to supply alcohol to a child who is a person under the age of 18 years.

4.4   Supply by under-age staff

It is an offence for any member or officer of the club, who is present in a capacity to prevent it, to allow a person under the age of 18 years to sell or supply alcohol on the club's premises unless that sale or supply has been authorised by that member or officer or another member or officer with the same responsibility (LA 2003, s 153).

There is an exception for the supply of alcohol to a member or guest for consumption with a table meal in a part of the club's premises set aside for the service of table meals and where alcohol is not sold or supplied except in conjunction with those table meals.

'Table meal' means 'a meal eaten by a person seated at a table, counter or other structure' not used for the service of other refreshments (LA 2003, s 159).

4.5   Unaccompanied children

Unaccompanied children, under the age of 16 years, are not permitted in premises used exclusively or primarily for the supply and consumption of alcohol. This prohibition applies equally to members' clubs. A child is unaccompanied if not in the company of someone aged 18 years or more.

It is an offence for members, officers and staff, in a position to prevent unaccompanied children being present in the premises, to allow children to be present (LA 2003, s 145).

Clearly this can cause problems for members' clubs with youth sections or under-16 sporting teams, and care must be taken to ensure that when such children are present they are not in parts of the premises being then used for the supply and consumption of alcohol. It would be permissible, therefore, to allow unaccompanied children into a part of the club set aside for table meals or in a bar area when the bar was closed.

No offence is committed if the child is simply passing through the premises when there is no other convenient means of access or egress.

A person charged with an offence under these provisions, by reason of that person's own conduct, has a defence if it can be shown that:

- the defendant believed the unaccompanied child was over the age of 16 or was accompanied by a person over the age of 18; and

- either the defendant had taken all reasonable steps to establish the individual's age, or nobody could reasonably have suspected from the individual's appearance that the individual was aged under 16 or 18 as the case may be.

A person is treated as having taken all reasonable steps to establish an individual's age if that person asked for evidence of age, and the evidence given would have convinced a reasonable person.

A members' club, its officers and staff have to give careful thought to arrangements for its own and visiting teams of under-age players. Whether or not a child is accompanied by a person who has attained the age of 18 would be a matter to be determined by the court dealing with any prosecution under the section. It would, as a matter of fact, be decided on the evidence adduced. An important influencing factor might be the extent to which the accompanying adult can be said to be supervising the behaviour and activities of any particular child.

If, for example, 15 under-age visiting rugby players and three reserves are found in a club bar during opening hours, in the company of one adult manager or coach, it might be stretching credulity to suggest that each one of the 15 was accompanied in the way demanded by the legislation. On the other hand, should two young golfers come into a club bar during opening hours in the company of the club professional or the club captain, a court might be persuaded that they were properly accompanied.

Finally, clubs might need to review their practices on presentation ceremonies. The hour set for the ceremony might be altered to make it possible for it to take place in the main bar. Alternatively, part of the club's premises that does not fall within the definition of 'relevant premises' might be used for the function. In an extreme case, a club might have to arrange for the awards to be given at a different venue, such as a meeting room in the local town hall.

4.6   Supply of alcohol to children

It is an offence to sell or supply alcohol to children under the age of 18 years (LA 2003, s 146).

Any person who supplied the alcohol or allowed the supply to take place is liable to be charged, and the club itself may also be prosecuted.

LA 2003, s 146 also provides that it is an offence to supply alcohol on behalf of a club:

- to, or to the order of, a member of the club who has not attained the age of 18; or

- to the order of an adult member of the club, for consumption by an individual who is aged under 18.

A club commits an offence if alcohol is supplied by it or on its behalf:

- to, or to the order of, a member of the club who is under 18; or

- on the order of an adult member of the club, to an individual who is under 18.

The statutory defences described below are available to persons or clubs charged with an offence under these provisions.

Just as it is offence for a club or a person to supply alcohol to an under-aged child, so it is an offence for any person or club to allow the supply of alcohol to a person who has not attained the age of 18 (LA 2003, s 147). Thus, it is an offence for a person, whether a member of the club, an officer or someone working at the club (whether paid or not), knowingly to allow alcohol to be supplied on relevant premises, by or on behalf of the club:

- to or to the order of a member who is under 18; or

- on the order of a member of the club, to an individual who is under 18.

The statutory defences do not apply to this offence because here the onus is on the prosecution to prove that the defendant knowingly allowed the supply. Further, any member or officer of the club who, at the time of the supply, was on the club premises in a capacity that enabled him to prevent that supply, may be guilty of the offence if that member or officer knew that the supply was being or was about to be made.

It is also an offence for a person to send a child to obtain alcohol from the club (LA 2003, s 152).

4.7 Purchase of alcohol by or on behalf of children

A child, under the age of 18 years, commits an offence where he is a member of a club and alcohol is supplied to him or to his order as a result of some act or default of his or he attempts to have alcohol supplied to him (LA 2003, s 149).

There is an exception for test purchases conducted on behalf of police officers or weights and measures inspectors (often trading standards officers).

It is also an offence for a person to buy or attempt to buy alcohol on behalf of a child or, where he is a member of a club, he makes arrangements or attempts to make arrangements for the supply to him or to his order of alcohol on behalf of a child.

Similarly, it is an offence for a member of a club to cause, by some act or default of his, alcohol to be supplied to him for consumption by a child or to attempt to have alcohol supplied to him for such consumption.

There is an exception for beer, wine or cider supplied to a child aged 16 or 17 years for consumption with a table meal and where that child is accompanied by a person of 18 years or more.

4.8 Consumption of alcohol by children

It is an offence for a child under the age of 18 years to consume alcohol in the premises of a club with a club premises certificate (LA 2003, s 150).

It is also an offence knowingly to allow a child to consume alcohol on club premises. The offence can be committed by anyone working at the club, whether paid or not, and any member or officer who is present at the time and has the capacity to prevent the consumption.

Although it might be a rare event, it is also an offence for a person who works at a club (whether paid or unpaid) to deliver alcohol or to allow alcohol to be delivered to a child under the age of 18 years (LA 2003, s 151). This provision does not apply to a situation where the alcohol is supplied or sold for consumption at the club because that would be caught by the law against sale or supply for consumption.

4.9   Supply of liqueur confectionery to children

It is a separate offence to sell or supply liqueur confectionary to children under the age of 16. The club also commits the offence if it supplies the liqueur confectionary to or to the order of a member who is under the age of 16 years or to the order of a member of the club to a child under the age of 16 (LA 2003, s 148).

The statutory defences set out below apply in such cases.

For these purposes, 'liqueur confectionery' means confectionery that contains alcohol in a proportion not greater than 0.2 litres of alcohol (of strength not exceeding 57%) per kilogramme of confectionery, consisting either of pieces weighing not more than 42 grammes or designed to be broken into such pieces for the purpose of consumption.

4.10   Exposing alcohol for unauthorised sale

Should club premises be used for unauthorised sales of alcohol an offence is committed by the person who exposes that alcohol for sale (LA 2003, s 137).

Whether the sale is authorised or not depends upon the club rules, the terms of the club premises certificate and the facts of each case.

A sale to a person who was neither a member nor the guest of a member would be caught by this provision.

The danger for members' clubs in falling foul of this provision is that a court has the power to order the alcohol and any container to be forfeited and destroyed.

4.11   Keeping alcohol on club premises for unauthorised sale

A person commits an offence if he has in his possession or under his control alcohol which he intends to sell by retail or supply where that activity would be an unauthorised licensable activity (LA 2003, s 138).

For the supply of alcohol to members and guests to be authorised it must be in accordance with the terms of the club premises certificate granted by the licensing authority.

If, for example, the certificate has a condition limiting the hours during which such supplies can be made, then a supply outside those hours would be an unauthorised licensable activity. So any supply would be a criminal offence of carrying on an unauthorised licensable activity and the keeping of the alcohol for such a supply would be an additional offence.

Again the real danger for a club is that the alcohol could be ordered to be forfeited and destroyed and proceedings could be taken against the club for a review of its certificate.

4.12   Allowing disorderly conduct on the premises

Every officer or member of a club, and any person employed in club premises, whether paid or unpaid, is under a duty to ensure that the premises are conducted in an orderly fashion. Consequently, should any such person knowingly allow disorderly conduct to occur, that person is guilty of an offence and liable to a fine (LA 2003, s 140).

This offence can be committed by any member or officer who was in the premises at the relevant time in a capacity which enabled the member or officer to prevent the disorderly conduct.

It is important to remember that, where such a charge is brought, it is for the prosecutor to prove, beyond reasonable doubt, that the defendant knew that the disorderly conduct was taking place. The offence is not an 'absolute' offence.

4.13   Supply of alcohol to a person who is drunk

LA 2003, s 141 prohibits the supply of alcohol to a person who has already had enough to make him drunk. It is an offence for any member or officer of a club, or any person who works in a club, whether paid or unpaid, knowingly to supply or attempt to supply alcohol to a person who is drunk.

It is also an offence for a person who is present on the premises in a capacity which enables that person to prevent it, knowingly to allow alcohol to be supplied to a drunken person.

4.14   Statutory defences

Many of the offences created by the LA 2003 are absolute offences or strict liability offences. In other words, they do not require proof of criminal intent. Such regulatory offences are justified on the basis of the social need. Where terms such as 'knowingly' are used, proof of intention is required before conviction.

In the case of strict liability offences the LA 2003 provides statutory defences for those whose actions whilst reasonable would otherwise result in their being convicted of criminal offences.

So LA 2003, s 139 provides for the offences of carrying out unauthorised licensable activities, exposing alcohol for unauthorised sale and keeping alcohol on premises for unauthorised sale, the defence that:

• the act was due to mistake, or to reliance on information given or to an act or omission by another person or some other cause beyond his control; and

• he took all reasonable precautions and exercised all due diligence to avoid committing the offence.

A court would decide, as a matter of fact, whether the defendant had taken all the precautions that could have been taken, and exercised as much care as was practicable. Evidence of systems put in place to prevent offences being committed and staff training and the effectiveness of those systems and training would assist a club and its officers in proving due diligence (see *Davies v Carmarthenshire County Council* [2005] EWHC 464 (Admin), [2005] LLR 276).

As seen above, a person charged with an offence relating to the sale or supply of alcohol to a child has the defence that he believed the person concerned was 18 years or older and that he had taken all reasonable steps to establish that individual's age or that nobody could have reasonably suspected from that person's appearance that he or she was aged under 18.

All reasonable steps to establish an individual's age are deemed by the Act to be taken if the person selling or supplying the alcohol has asked for proof of age and the evidence provided would have convinced a reasonable person.

4.15   Inspections and powers of entry and search

When an application for a club premises certificate is made, or an application for the variation or review of such a certificate is made, a constable authorised by the chief officer of police, and other authorised persons, are entitled to enter and inspect the premises to which the certificate relates (LA 2003, s 96).

Any such entry and inspection must take place at a reasonable time, on a day not more than 14 days after the making of the application. The Act stipulates that a person wishing to inspect premises under these powers must give at least 48 hours' notice of the intended visit to the club; the notice must specify the time and date at which it is intended to carry out the inspection.

The licensing authority may extend the time limit for making such an inspection, on the application of a responsible authority, but by not more than 7 days. An extension of time may be granted only if it appears to the licensing authority that reasonable steps for an inspection to be made in good time were made, but that it was not possible for it to take place within the time allowed.

Any person who obstructs an authorised person or a constable in their exercise of these powers of entry and inspection is guilty of an offence.

In addition to the powers of entry and inspection mentioned above, LA 2003, s 97 gives police constables a general right to enter and search club premises in certain circumstances. This right may be exercised only if the officer has reasonable cause to believe that:

- an offence under Misuse of Drugs Act 1971, s 4(3)(a), (b) or (c) has been, is being, or is about to be, committed there (these are offences of supplying or offering to supply, or being concerned in supplying or making an offer to supply, a controlled drug); or

- there is likely to be a breach of the peace there.

In these circumstances the officer may, if necessary, use reasonable force to gain entry.

4.16   Smuggled goods

The relaxation of import controls following European Community agreements have made it possible for unscrupulous people to bring large quantities of alcohol into the country with the object of selling it on to pubs, clubs and off-licences. Much publicised 'booze cruises' are the source of many of these illegal operations. Club officers should exercise extreme caution to avoid the possibility of purchasing any such smuggled goods. It is a serious offence to keep smuggled goods on club premises.

LA 2003, s 144 provides that the offence is committed if any person knowingly keeps, or allows to be kept, on any relevant premises, any goods which have been imported without payment of duty or which have otherwise been unlawfully imported.

In the case of premises that have the benefit of a club premises certificate, any member or officer of the club present on the premises when smuggled goods are kept there, in a capacity that enables the member or officer to prevent them from being so kept, may be charged with the offence.

5   Temporary Events

5.1   Introduction

From time to time, a members' club may find that it wishes to stage an event that cannot conveniently be held in its usual premises. The club may wish to boost its finances by holding a summer barbecue or a New Year Ball, or it may arrange prize presentation evenings that will attract greater numbers than can be accommodated comfortably in the club's certified premises.

Alternatively, there may be occasions when the club wishes to use its own premises for purposes that are outside the limitations of the club's premises certificate.

5.2   Temporary event notices

LA 2003, Pt 5 makes provisions for temporary activities known as temporary events.

If a club wishes to use alternative premises for licensable activities during any period that does not exceed 96 hours, a notice may be given to the relevant licensing authority that a temporary event is to be held there.

The relevant licensing authority is the licensing authority for the area in which the premises where the event is to be held are situated. Thus it may be a different authority from the one which granted the club premises certificate.

If the club, or anyone else wishes to use the club's premises for a function which is outside the limitations of the club's premises certificate, again a notice may be given to the licensing authority.

The provisions in relation to temporary events apply only if the number of persons expected to attend at any one time during the event is less than 500.

Where the licensable activities at the event will include the supply of alcohol, it must be a condition of the notice that such supplies are to be made by or under the authority of the premises user.

An individual may give up to five temporary event notices in any year. No more than 12 notices may be given in respect of the same premises within the same year.

These limits are different for a holder of a 'personal licence' under the Act; but a club member or officer would not normally hold such a licence.

There must always be a gap of at least 24 hours between the end of one event period and the commencement of the next.

Temporary event procedures are not appropriate where a club needs to find alternative premises for an extended period, for example, while the club premises are being refurbished. If a club needs to use alternative premises for a continuous period in excess of 96 hours, the club must make an application under s 84, for the variation of the club premises certificate (see Chapter 3). On completion of the works, a further application must be made to vary the certificate once more so that it relates to the original club premises.

5.3   (Application) Giving a temporary event notice

A temporary event notice should be given by an individual, so, in the case of a members' club, it is convenient for the secretary or the member who is organising the event to give the required notice. The person who gives the notice becomes the 'premises user' for the purposes of the event. A person giving a temporary event notice must be over the age of 18.

Two copies of the temporary event notice must be served on the relevant licensing authority no later than 10 working days before the day on which the event period begins. The notice must be in a prescribed form (downloadable from the DCMS website or obtainable from the local licensing authority). It must be accompanied by the appropriate fee.

If the form is sent to the licensing authority electronically by the approved means it is up to the authority to send a copy to the police no later than the end of the working day after notice was given to the authority. Otherwise the giver of the notice must give a copy to the police not less than 10 working days before the day when the event is to begin.

The licensing authority must acknowledge receipt of the duplicate notices by sending one to the premises user so marked within one working day of its receipt of the notice.

5.4   Police objection

The police may object to the event if they are of the opinion that allowing the premises to be used in accordance with the notice would undermine the crime prevention objective of the legislation. This is the only ground upon which the police may object. Any notice of objection must be given to the licensing authority no later than 48 hours after the date on which the chief officer is given a copy of the event notice.

Where notice of objection is given, the licensing authority must hold a hearing to consider the objection. Having held the hearing, the authority may consider it necessary, in the interests of promoting the crime prevention objective, to give a counter notice. A counter notice must be given to the premises user at least 24 hours before the beginning of the specified event period. If it is given within this time limit, the effect is that the premises user is prohibited from staging the event.

In some circumstances the police may, before the hearing, discuss their concerns with the premises user with a view to agreeing modifications to the temporary event notice which would meet the concerns of the police while allowing the event to proceed. Such an agreement may be reached at any time before a hearing is held to consider the police objection. Where such modifications are agreed, the notice of objection is withdrawn and the hearing is not necessary.

5.5   Checklist

- The applicant must be over 18 years of age.

- The event period must not exceed 96 hours.

- If there is to be more than one event, at least 24 hours must elapse between the end of one and the commencement of another.

- Notice must be given to the relevant licensing authority not less than 10 working days before the beginning of the event period.

- The event notice must include a condition that the supply of alcohol is to be under the authority of the premises user.

- The appropriate fee must be sent with the notice.

5.6   Rights of entry

Constables and authorised officers (of a licensing authority) may enter premises to which a temporary event notice applies for the purpose of assessing the likely effect of the event on the promotion of the crime prevention objective. An authorised officer must produce evidence of authority to exercise the power if requested to do so.

It is an offence for any person intentionally to obstruct an authorised officer exercising this power. The maximum penalty is a fine not exceeding £500.

5.7   The temporary event notice

The receipted temporary event notice returned to the premises user by the licensing authority is the authorisation for the event.

When premises are being used on the authority of a temporary event notice, the premises user is under a duty to make sure that a copy of that notice is prominently displayed at the premises, or that the notice is in his custody or in the custody of another person, nominated for this purpose, who is working at the premises.

Where such a nomination has been made, a notice of that fact, and the position held by the person who has been so nominated, must be prominently displayed at the premises. Failure to comply with these requirements is an offence; the maximum penalty is a fine not exceeding £500.

If the temporary event notice is not displayed at the event premises (and no notice as to the designated custodian of the notice is posted on them), a constable or authorised officer may require the premises user to produce the temporary event notice for examination. Again, if asked to do so, an authorised officer must produce evidence of authority to exercise this power. Failure, without reasonable excuse, to produce a temporary event notice in accordance with a requirement made in this way is an offence. The maximum penalty is a fine not exceeding £500.

Even in the best ordered of organisations things can go wrong. However carefully important papers are guarded, it is still possible for them to be mislaid or misappropriated. The legislation acknowledges that fact and makes provision for duplicate documents to be obtained. LA 2003, s 110 makes provision for obtaining duplicate temporary event notices upon payment of the requisite fee. The licensing authority is under a duty to supply the certified copy requested if it is satisfied that the original has been lost, stolen, damaged or destroyed and, where it has been lost or stolen, that the loss or theft has been reported to the police. These provisions may be important because the documents in question have to be produced when applications are made, or on the request of a police constable or an authorised officer of the licensing authority.

A copy issued under these provisions must be a copy of the document in the form in which it existed immediately before it was lost, stolen, damaged or destroyed. This requirement underscores the importance of the authority's duty, under s 93, to keep its records up to date.

6 Entertainment

6.1 Introduction

Under the LA 2003 a club that wishes, or may wish, to provide regulated entertainment should, when applying for a club premises certificate, include the relevant entertainment(s) in the list of qualifying activities to be allowed under the club premises certificate.

LA 2003, Sch 1 concerns the provision of regulated entertainment or entertainment facilities, either exclusively for members of a qualifying club, or for the members of such a club and their guests.

6.2 Regulated entertainments

The entertainments within the provisions of the schedule are:

- a performance of a play;
- an exhibition of a film;
- an indoor sporting event;
- a boxing or wrestling entertainment;
- a performance of live music;
- any playing of recorded music;
- a performance of dance;
- live music, recorded music or dance which takes place in the presence of an audience and is provided wholly or partly to entertain that audience.

The entertainment facilities within the schedule are:

- making music;
- dancing; and
- other similar entertainment.

'Music' includes vocal or instrumental music or any combination of the two.

Poetry readings and performances by stand-up comedians (which do not involve music) are not regulated by the LA 2003.

In relation to the provision of regulated entertainment, there are a number of exemptions, as follows.

6.2.1   Films

The showing of films is not to be regarded as the provision of a regulated entertainment if the sole or main purpose is to demonstrate a product, advertise goods or services or provide information, education or instruction. A similar exemption applies to films shown in museums or art galleries.

6.2.2   Incidental music

Live or recorded music is exempt, provided it is incidental to some other activity that is not itself an entertainment or the provision of an entertainment facility regulated by the LA 2003. So, for example, the playing of background music (musak) or the playing of a pianist in a restaurant for the benefit of the diners would not be regulated.

6.3   New applications

In the case of a members' club applying for a new club premises certificate, the provision of entertainment should be included as a qualifying activity which the club wishes to be allowed to engage in, when the club operating schedule is completed. The activities specified in the schedule will, as a general rule, be translated into the permitted qualifying activities authorised under the certificate.

If the provision of entertainment is not included, an application for the variation of the club premises certificate will have to be made should the club wish, subsequently, to provide it. See Chapter 3 for a more detailed explanation of the procedure for making such applications.

6.4   Licences to use copyright works

Clubs which provide entertainment by live performers, discotheques, electronic reproduction of sound such as by compact discs, television or a juke box, are not free to provide that entertainment simply because they have a club premises certificate.

Copyright licences may have to be obtained and fees paid to the organisations that look after the interests of the artistes responsible for the creation of such entertainment and those who produce it and have copyright interests in the material. The principal bodies in question are the Performing Right Society and Phonographic Performance Ltd. Many clubs provide entertainment illegally, simply because they do not know about their obligations to pay fees to these bodies. In respect of music videos, licences may be required from the Mechanical Copyright Protection Society and/or Video Performance Ltd.

6.4.1   Performing Right Society

The function of the Performing Right Society is to safeguard the rights of composers and lyricists in relation to the public performance of their works. The Society levies fees for the right to give such public performances and the fees raised are distributed to those who composed the music or songs performed. Several different tariffs apply, depending on how the copyright material is used. Members' clubs come within a tariff known as the Joint Members' Clubs (JMC) tariff.

The fees charged change from time to time. The JMC tariff applies to performances of copyright music within the Society's repertoire at clubs bona fide established and conducted in good faith as non-profit-making members' clubs capable of qualifying for a club premises certificate. It does not apply to proprietary clubs.

If a club applies for and obtains the Society's licence before musical performances commence, the standard royalty rate is payable in respect of the first year of the licence. If the music user does not obtain a licence before musical performances commence, the higher royalty rate (standard plus 50%) is payable for the first year of the licence. In either case, at the end of the first year, the standard royalty rate is charged and payable.

6.4.2   Featured recorded music

For all performances by record, compact disc or tape player primarily for entertainment by means of discotheque equipment or otherwise for dancing and karaoke performances, there is a standard royalty per performance for the first 100 persons present. For each additional 25 persons, or part of such number, there is an additional fee (royalty). But where performances of this type are given at a function, such as a wedding reception or a 21st birthday party, and in the same room as the function the rates are reduced.

6.4.3   Annual licence for featured music

Alternatively, the club may apply for an annual licence. Again, there are standard and higher rates. Where, however, there are no more than three functions in a licence year, these rates are not charged. In such cases, there is a set charge for each function.

6.4.4 Cinema and featured video

For showing films, DVDs or videos in a room or place specially used for video or cinema exhibition, and with seating arranged accordingly, again there is a royalty charge for the first 100 people in attendance with an additional payment per 25 people.

6.4.5 Background or mechanical music

There are annual royalties for the use of broadcast or music playing equipment:

* television (without video) depending upon the size of screen;

* radio – per set;

* video player (with or without television facilities through the same screen) except performances where there are special seating arrangements for viewing, or when the player is used for discotheque performances – again depending upon the size of the screen;

* record, compact disc or tape player, or music centre – where two or more such instruments or screens are used in the same premises, whether of the same or of different kinds, the combined charges for the instruments is reduced by 10%;

* jukeboxes – depending upon their facilities (eg with or without background music facilities) and the number of coin entry points;

* video jukeboxes – depending upon the size of screen and background facilities;

* combined audio/video jukeboxes.

Value added tax is payable on all royalties charged.

For details of the current rates for royalties and licences the Performing Right Society should be contacted. The Society has a very helpful website at www.prsformusic.com.

'Capacity' is calculated as follows: where the accommodation of a room is limited to the number of seats, the capacity is calculated by reference to the total number of seats. Where, as in the case of discotheque performances, there is no formal means of calculating the accommodation of a room, capacity is assessed by reference to the maximum number of persons who can reasonably be accommodated in the room, or which is permitted under any regulation by the fire authority or under the club's rules.

Forms of application for licences are obtainable from the Society whose offices are at 29–33 Berners Street, London W1P 4AA. Advice can be obtained by phone on 020 7580 5544. Its website address is www.prs.co.uk. Arrangements can also be made for Society inspectors to visit club premises to assess the club's needs and advise on appropriate fees. Inspectors are able to issue licences at the time of visiting.

6.4.6   Phonographic Performance Limited

Clubs which provide musical entertainment may also have to obtain a licence from Phonographic Performance Ltd (PPL). This may seem strange when fees are also payable to the Performing Right Society, but there are two quite separate copyrights in each sound recording. The songwriter or composer owns the copyright in the song, and licence fees in respect of that copyright are collected by the Performing Right Society. The copyright in the recording is owned by the record company which financed and produced it, and its licence fees are collected by PPL.

PPL levies its fees in advance. This is because permission must be obtained before the performance takes place. Once the appropriate fee has been paid, PPL issues its licence fairly quickly. The fee payable is based entirely on the information the applicant provides about its public use of sound recordings. Once PPL has that information, it determines which of its charging tariffs is appropriate. The company says that by relating licence fees very specifically to the actual use made of sound recordings, it can ensure that the applicant is not overcharged.

PPL has its offices at 1 Upper James Street, London W1F 9DE and advice can be obtained from the company by phone on 020 7534 1000. The company's website address is www. ppluk.com.

6.5   Film and television screening

6.5.1   Films

Great care has to be taken by a members' club wishing to screen films for members and guests. First, before it may exhibit a film on the club premises, the club's premises certificate must include the exhibition of films as one of the qualifying activities. Where the certificate does authorise the exhibition of films, the authorisation must be subject to the condition that restricts the admission of children in accordance with LA 2003, s 74. That section provides that if a 'film classification body' (in effect, the British Board of Film Classification) is specified in the certificate, admission must, generally, be restricted in accordance with any recommendation made by the Board. For example, if a film is classified as a film for exhibition to persons over the age of 15, children under that age may not be admitted to the performance. If the British Board of Film Classification is not specified in the premises certificate, or the licensing authority has notified the club that admission is to be restricted in accordance with any recommendation made by the authority itself, then the authority's own restrictions, if any, must be respected. For example, if the authority has applied an '18' classification to the film, persons under that age must be excluded.

Some thought must also be given to the source of the films that are to be shown. Films that are rented or purchased from a retail outlet cannot be shown. Copyright laws restrict the screening of such films to the home. Films may be screened for the members of a club only if they have been obtained from a non-theatrical distributor who provides the club with a copyright licence.

Care must also be taken to ensure that the club is not acting as a 'cinema'. The films that are shown in the club must not be advertised outside the premises and the general public must not be admitted to performances of the film in return for an entrance fee.

The Federation Against Copyright Theft (FACT) acts as the regulating body for the film industry. It monitors activities such as piracy and illegal screenings. Prosecutions arising from investigations by this body can lead to the imposition of substantial fines.

Further information about the screening of films in members' clubs can be obtained from FACT, which has offices at 7 Victory Business Centre, Worton Road, Isleworth, Middlesex TW7 6DB. The phone number is 020 8568 6646 and the website address is www.fact-uk.org.uk.

Information about hiring films for screening in club premises can be obtained from Filmbank Distributors Ltd, 98 Theobalds Road, London WC1X 8WB; phone 020 7984 5958; www.filmbank.co.uk.

6.5.2   Television programmes

The simultaneous reception and playing of a television programme does not constitute 'regulated entertainment' for the purposes of the LA 2003. Members' clubs should, though, exercise caution when contemplating screening televised programmes such as major sporting events. To receive transmissions from terrestrial television companies the club must have a television licence for its premises. In the case of satellite transmissions, the club needs the appropriate authority from the satellite broadcasting company.

Sky Television issues viewing cards that authorise the reception of its transmissions. The company does not issue the same cards for all types of premises. Organisations such as members' clubs are not allowed to screen transmissions using a viewing card sold to an individual member. The charge Sky makes for authority to receive transmissions depends on the programme(s) in question. Details of the fees that would be charged to a members' club can be supplied by Sky TV; www.business.sky.com. Fees generally reflect the appeal of the programmes that are to be shown and the size of the potential audience.

6.6   Plays

Some clubs may have occasion to stage plays on club premises. Once again, a club that wishes, or may wish, to do so should include this activity in the club operating schedule submitted with the application for a club premises certificate. The performance of plays will then be included as one of the club's qualifying activities.

LA 2003, s 76 provides that the licensing authority may impose conditions on the certificate in relation to the performance of plays only if it considers it necessary to do so in the interests of public safety. Conditions might, for example, prohibit the use of naked flames during productions, or the number of persons who might appear on stage at any one time. The type of play to be performed, or the content of the plays, may not be the subject of conditions attaching to the premises certificate.

6.7   Bingo

Whilst a form of entertainment, Bingo is also a form of gambling for which a separate authority is required (see Chapter 7).

6.8   Sexual entertainment

Some members' clubs have a long tradition of providing sexual entertainment such as striptease, whilst others will cater occasionally for hen and stag parties. Prior to April 2010 such entertainment could be provided using the authority of a club premises certificate, provided the certificate included authority to provide music and dancing.

In 2010 the law was changed so that, provided the relevant local authority had resolved to adopt the provisions of the Local Government

(Miscellaneous Provisions) Act 1982 in its area, those providing sexual entertainment in the form of striptease, table dancing or lap dancing had to apply for a sexual entertainment venue licence.

A 'sexual entertainment venue' is defined in Local Government (Miscellaneous Provisions) Act 1982, Sch 3 as:

> ... any premises at which relevant entertainment is provided before a live audience for the financial gain of the organiser or the entertainer

And 'relevant entertainment' means:

(a) any live performance; or

(b) any live display of nudity;

> which is of such a nature that, ignoring financial gain, it must reasonably be assumed to be provided solely or principally for the purpose of sexually stimulating any member of the audience (whether by verbal or other means).

'Audience' includes an audience of one.

'Display of nudity' means:

(a) in the case of a woman, exposure of her nipples, pubic area, genitals or anus; and

(b) in the case of a man, exposure of his pubic area, genitals or anus.

'The organiser' in relation to the provision of relevant entertainment at premises means any person who is responsible for the management of:

(c) the relevant entertainment; or

(d) the premises.

Whilst in relation to a bona fide members' club it could be argued that the organiser does not receive any financial gain, it is unlikely that the same can be argued for the entertainer(s) so that a licence for a sex establishment under the Local Government (Miscellaneous Provisions) Act 1982 will be needed if a club wishes to provide sexual entertainment.

There is provision for a limited number of such events, no more than 11 per year, without the need for a licence but those events must be at least a calendar month apart.

If sexual entertainment is to be provided on more than 11 days in a calendar year then the organiser of the events will have to apply for a licence.

6.9   Sex establishment licence

An application for a sex establishment licence has to be made to the local authority in which the club premises are situated by the organiser of the sexual entertainment. A licence can only be granted to a person, including a body corporate, and not an association, club or unincorporated body.

The application form can be obtained from the local authority. If the authority grants the licence it lasts for one year and then has to be renewed. The local authority can impose such conditions as it thinks appropriate. The licence can be transferred to another person on the application of that person and may be renewed.

Public notice, by advertising in a local newspaper, has to be given within 7 days of making the application to the local authority and a notice has to be displayed at the premises where it can be seen and read by members of the public. A copy of the application must be served on the police.

The local authority must refuse a sex establishment licence on the grounds that the applicant is under 18, not resident in the United Kingdom, has been disqualified or is acting on behalf of a person who is disqualified. In addition, the local authority has a discretion to refuse the licence because of the unsuitability of the applicant, that the number of sex establishments already in the locality equals or exceeds the number previously fixed by the local authority, or that it would be inappropriate to grant or renew the licence because of the character of the locality, the use to which any premises in the locality are put or the character and layout of the premises.

A local authority can resolve that the number of sex establishment licences in a particular area shall be 'nil' but it is doubtful whether such a decision could be made for the whole of the authority's area rather than designated parts of it.

It is an offence to be involved in the organisation of sexual entertainment without a licence. Children under 18 are not permitted to enter or to work in such premises.

Police officers and authorised local authority officers have the power to enter and inspect premises subject to a sex establishment licence for the purpose of ensuring that the establishment is being run in accordance with conditions imposed on the licence.

PART TWO

GAMBLING

7 Gambling

7.1 Introduction

Special provisions relate to gambling in premises where alcohol is sold or supplied. Members' clubs have some distinct advantages compared with public houses and other licensed premises.

The Gambling Act 2005, as with previous legislation, seeks to control gambling not by making forms of gambling illegal but by controlling the circumstances in which gambling can take place.

Gambling is defined in the Gambling Act 2005 as gaming, betting and participating in a lottery. In turn, gaming means playing a game of chance for a prize and that includes a game that involves both an element of chance and an element of skill, a game that involves an element of chance that can be eliminated by superlative skill and a game that is presented as involving an element of chance but does not include the playing of a sport.

No bankers' games such as pontoon or blackjack, roulette and other games that involve staking against the holder of the bank are allowed to be played in members' clubs unless the club has the benefit of a club gaming permit.

A club may not be established for the purpose of gaming save for the playing of bridge or whist.

The Gambling Commission has published a Code of Practice for those offering facilities for equal chance gaming in members' clubs. The Code requires that clubs designate a person to supervise the gaming to make sure, for example, that those under 18 are not allowed to participate. Clubs are expected to keep separate records of the payment of participation fees, amounts staked and prize money. Facilities and equipment provided for gaming should be that of the club and rules should be clearly displayed. All members' clubs should obtain a copy of the Code which can be downloaded from the Gambling Commission's website.

7.2   Betting

Betting conducted with bookmakers is not allowed in members' clubs and the provision of facilities to bet in clubs would be illegal. Similarly, a member of staff must not act as a conduit through whom bets can be forwarded to a bookmaker. Any member of staff so acting would be treated as a betting intermediary and liable to prosecution.

There is nothing to stop a club providing facilities for watching sport on television and if members and their guest wish to bet by using their own phones to contact their own bookmakers, that would be quite lawful. But for the club to provide a dedicated phone line or the use of a mobile phone for the purposes of betting would be illegal.

7.3   Bingo

The playing of bingo by members and their bona fide guests has become a tradition in members' clubs and miners' welfare institutes. Special rules apply to such clubs which enable the clubs to make small charges for playing bingo. Different charges may be made depending upon whether the club has the benefit of a club gaming permit or not.

A members' club may apply to the local authority for a club gaming permit which, if granted, will allow a club to offer other forms of equal chance gaming with unlimited stakes and prizes.

With a club gaming permit the club can charge up to £3 per day for participation.

Bingo can be played in members' clubs that do not have club gaming permits. In such circumstances there is a maximum charge of £1 per day for participation.

In both sets of circumstances there is a maximum stake of £5 per player per game and the total stakes and/or prizes must not exceed £2,000 per week save for one occasion each year.

The club is not allowed to make any deduction from either the charges (stakes) for playing each game or the prize funds.

If the stakes/prizes will exceed £2,000 per week then the club must apply to the Gambling Commission for a bingo operating licence such as that granted to commercial bingo clubs.

7.4   Poker

Poker may be played in members' clubs but unless the club has the benefit of a club gaming permit there are strict limits upon stakes and prizes.

Without a club gaming permit the limits on poker are for the total stakes – £1,000 per week but no more than £250 per day and no more than £10 per person per game. The limits on prizes are £250 per game. The club can charge a participation fee of £1 per day. The playing of poker in the form of poker leagues is subject to the same limits so that if the overall winner has played in three games, including the final, then the maximum prize money must not exceed £750 (3 x £250). Any additional prizes would have a monetary value and that would have to be taken into account to ensure that the limit is not exceeded.

If the club has the benefit of a club gaming permit there is no limit on either stakes or prizes and the club can charge a participation fee of £3 per day.

7.5   Other forms of gaming

Save for Pontoon and Chemin-de-Fer where the club has a club gaming permit, all forms of bankers' or unequal chance gaming are prohibited.

Save for Bingo and Poker (see above) equal chance gaming is allowed without limit on stakes or prizes.

As with Bingo and Poker the maximum participation charge that the club can make is £1 per day unless the club has a club gaming permit when the maximum charge is £3.

7.6   Bridge and Whist

The Gambling Act 2005 makes provision for those wishing to play competitive Bridge and Whist to form members' clubs for that purpose. Such clubs may obtain club gaming permits and can then charge £20 per day in participation fees.

Members' clubs may also provide facilities for playing Bridge and Whist because they are forms of equal chance gaming. Clubs can charge participation fees of £18 on a day when no other gaming facilities are being provided. Otherwise, the participation fee is restricted to £1 or £3 if a club gaming permit is held.

7.7   Lotteries and competitions

Lotteries and competitions are frequent mechanisms for fund raising. They are dealt with in Chapter 8.

7.8   Gaming machines

Gaming machines are regulated by type or category. The number and type of such machines that can be sited in a club is restricted according to whether the club has a club gaming permit or a club machine permit or not. Clubs with a club gaming permit do not need a club machine permit in addition.

Clubs with a club gaming permit or a club machine permit may site up to three gaming machines from either categories B3A, B4, C or D but only one B3A machine can be sited.

Clubs without either permit are entitled to site two gaming machines from categories C or D.

7.9   Members and bona fide guests

For the purposes of gaming, a member must have been a member of the club for 48 hours before participating in gaming. Any guest who participates in gaming must have had a previous acquaintance with the member who introduced him or her and must not have been invited to attend the club only to enable him to use the gambling facilities provided.

7.10   Applications for club gaming permits and club machine permits

Gambling Act 2005, Sch 12 covers applications for club gaming permits and club machine permits. Applications must be made to the licensing authority (the local authority for the area in which the club is situated). The application must be made on the prescribed form (obtainable from the local authority or downloadable from the Gambling Commission's website). Schedule 12 sets out the information to be provided with the form which must also be accompanied by the set fee.

The information to be provided is set out in the application form and governed by the Gambling Act 2005 (Club Gaming and Club Machine Permits) Regulations 2007 (SI 2007/1834).

A copy of the application form must be sent to the Gambling Commission and the police within 7 days. Both have the right to object within 28 days setting out the reasons for their objections.

The licensing authority must refuse a permit if the club is not a qualifying club or miners' welfare institute or if the premises are used mainly by children or young persons. An application may also be refused if:

- the applicant has a previous gaming related conviction;

- gaming has been conducted in the premises which was unlawful or in breach of any of the conditions attached to a gaming permit;

- a gaming permit has been cancelled within the previous 10 years, or

- the police or Gambling Commission has objected to the grant (or renewal) of the permit.

If the police or the Gambling Commission object, there must be a hearing before the licensing authority unless the parties consent to the dispensation of such a requirement for a hearing.

There is no power to attach additional conditions to the grant of a club gaming permit or club machine permit.

The licensing authority must inform the applicant and police and Gambling Commission of their decision as soon as reasonably practicable and give their reasons.

Where the club holds a club premises certificate for the sale of alcohol, there is a fast track procedure under which the licensing authority must grant the application unless an objection is received and the police or the Gambling Commission may not object save in limited circumstances, such as the use or proposed use of the premises for unlawful gambling or the fact that a previous permit has been cancelled within the last 10 years.

A permit lasts for 10 years unless it lapses, is surrendered, cancelled or forfeited. A fast track permit lasts indefinitely as long as the club premises certificate remains in force. There is an annual fee for each permit. Failure to pay the annual fee will result in the permit being cancelled unless the failure to pay can be shown to have been the result of an administrative error.

Where a permit requires renewal, the application for renewal must be made not earlier than 3 months and not later than 6 weeks before the expiry date. There is no power to extend this period or to accept late applications.

The club must keep the permit at the premises and produce it for inspection on the request of a police constable or enforcement officer of the licensing authority.

There are provisions allowing the variation of the permit if it ceases to be accurate.

If a permit is lost, stolen or damaged, an application can be made to the licensing authority for a replacement copy which must be granted provided the authority is satisfied that the permit has been lost, stolen or damaged and, if the former, that the loss or theft has been reported to the police.

The licensing authority has the power to cancel a permit if satisfied that the premises are used wholly or mainly by children or young persons or that an offence or a breach of the conditions of the permit has been committed. Again, a hearing will be necessary and reasons for any decision to cancel must be given. Any cancellation would not take effect until either the time allowed to lodge an appeal has passed or the appeal, if lodged, has been determined.

A court which convicts the holder of a club gaming permit or club machine permit may order forfeiture of the permit on such terms (including suspension) as the court deems appropriate in addition to any other sentence.

An appeal lies against a refusal to grant or renew a club gaming permit or club machine permit or to cancel such a permit to the local magistrates' court. An appeal against a court order of forfeiture lies to the Crown Court.

PART THREE

FUND RAISING

8 Fund Raising

8.1 Introduction

Clubs will use many different forms of fund raising, such as allowing their car parks to be used for car boot sales, to assist with meeting the costs of running the club. In this chapter we look at two particular forms that require special attention to avoid contravention of the Gambling Act 2005.

8.2 Lotteries

Lotteries can themselves take different forms, from simple draws or raffles to what appear at first sight to be competitions.

All lotteries for which you have to pay to enter are illegal unless conducted in accordance with the provisions of the Gambling Act 2005.

The definition of a simple lottery is given in Gambling Act 2005, s 14. It is that there has to be:

* a payment for taking part;

* at least one prize;

* prizes are awarded purely by chance.

So sweepstakes, say on the Grand National or Derby, tombolas, 100 clubs, football cards, scratch cards and prize draws are all forms of lotteries.

Lotteries can take more complex forms with the winners at a first stage going through to later stages with the chance of winning bigger prizes, for example. Those complex forms are still lotteries, provided the first of the processes relies wholly on chance.

8.3 Offences

If a lottery is unlawful, anyone involved in the promotion of the lottery commits an offence. Promotion includes making or taking part in the arrangements for the lottery. For example, making arrangements for the printing of lottery tickets, advertising the lottery and selling the tickets are all forms of promotion. Use of the club premises for an unlawful lottery would mean that all those involved in allowing that use are guilty of promotion.

8.4   Permitted lotteries

Certain types of lottery, not run for 'commercial purposes' that is not run for private gain, are permitted under the Gambling Act 2005. Those in which lottery tickets or chances are sold to members of the public must be registered either with the local authority or the Gambling Commission depending upon their size.

A society or club is a non-commercial society if it is established and conducted for:

• charitable purposes;

• the purpose of enabling participation in or of supporting sports, athletics or a cultural activity; or

• any other non-commercial purpose other than private gain.

The provision of benefit for one or more members of the club is not a provision for the purposes of private gain if made in the course of the activities of the non-commercial society or club.

Most members' clubs such as working men's clubs and sports clubs were formed for non-commercial purposes.

8.5   Incidental non-commercial lotteries

If the club is holding an event such as a dinner dance, a fete, a presentation of awards night or a sports contest, a lottery which is incidental to the event can be organised.

All tickets or chances must be sold at the event and the draw must take place at the event. There is a maximum prize limit of £500 and no more than £100 may be spent on the organisation of the lottery (such as printing costs).

8.6   Private society lottery

Members of a club not run for commercial purposes may organise what is known as a 'private society lottery' under Gambling Act 2005, Sch 11, Pt 2. A private society lottery is one run only by members of the society in which tickets are sold only to members of the society or on the club premises.

Any advertising can be done only at the club's premises and adverts must not be sent to any other premises. Tickets have to be in documentary form and are not transferable. Each ticket must be for the same price and payment must be made in full. Tickets must state the name and address of the promoters of the lottery and must specify to whom the tickets can be sold.

The promotion of the lottery must be authorised by the club, in writing. Where the club has branches or sections, each separate one is deemed to be a society for the purposes of promoting private society lotteries. So a big club with say a football section and a cricket section could authorise those individual sections to run their own private society lotteries.

There is no limit on how long the lottery can run for but each one must be a 'one-off' lottery and rollovers are not allowed. The costs of running the lottery and prizes can be deducted from the prize fund.

8.7   Small society lotteries

A 'small society lottery' in which the proceeds do not exceed £20,000 can be held by or on behalf of a members' club. The relevant provisions are set out in Gambling Act 2005, Sch 11, Pt 4.

'Proceeds' means the result of ticket sales. There is a limit of £250,000 for each calendar year on the total proceeds of small society lotteries held by a club or society. All the profits from the lottery must be for the benefit of the club or society and not for private gain. At least 25% of the proceeds must go to fund raising.

Rollovers are allowed but the maximum prize that anyone can win is £25,000.

Tickets must be in documentary form and state the society or club's name, the name and address of the promoter (a designated member of the club or member of staff or an external lottery manager) and the date of the draw. The price of each ticket must be the same and the money for the ticket must be paid at the time of sale. Tickets must not be sold to those under 16. There are different local restrictions as to whether tickets can be sold in public places, for example in the street. Careful checks must be made with the local authority, therefore, before tickets sales are made in public places.

To promote such a lottery, the club must register with the local authority for its area in accordance with Sch 11, Pt 5 and must remain registered throughout the period during which the lottery is promoted. With registration comes a requirement to file records with the authority from time to time.

There are provisions for much larger society lotteries for which an operating licence is needed. Such licences are granted by the Gambling Commission and normally relate to national societies. Large Society lotteries are not dealt with in this book.

Application forms for registration for a small society lottery can be obtained from the local authority. The purposes of the club must be made clear. The local authority must keep a register and notify the Gambling Commission of any registration. The only grounds for refusing registration are that:

- in the preceding 5 years an operating licence has been revoked or refused by the Gambling Commission;

- the club is deemed to be a commercial society (that is operated for private gain);

- somebody who will or may be connected with the promotion of the lottery has been convicted of one of the offences listed in Gambling Act 2005, Sch 7; or

- the applicant club or society has provided false or misleading information.

Once registered, an annual fee must be paid to the local authority. Registration can be revoked on any of the grounds upon which it could have been refused in the first place.

There is an appeal against refusal to grant or revocation to the local magistrates' court.

8.8   Prize competitions

Competitions as a way of raising funds are not made illegal by the Gambling Act 2005. A genuine prize competition is one where the outcome is determined by the application of skill, judgment or knowledge.

Under the law prior to the implementation of the Gambling Act 2005 many so-called prize competitions were in fact lotteries and were, therefore, illegal. The police and local authorities had far more pressing matters to deal with and so very few of the promoters of these illegal lotteries were prosecuted. The government's aim in changing the law was to allow such competitions by treating them as free lotteries, provided the cost of entry was no more than the cost of normal rate of communication or that if there was a small entry charge there was also an equally fair free entry route.

Many clubs run competitions for prizes. Such competitions are perfectly legal, provided the initial process for determining the winner is such as to either deter a significant proportion of those who wish to enter from doing so, or prevent a significant proportion of those taking part from winning a prize. In other words, provided the initial stage of the competition is not, in reality, a lottery then the competition should be lawful.

Care has to be taken, however, to ensure that the competition does not amount to a form of betting. As can be seen in Chapter 7, betting with bookmakers is not allowed in places where alcohol is sold or supplied.

Winning a prize for a sporting event is excluded from the definition of gaming.

8.9   Race nights

In the past, race nights have proved to be a popular form of fund raising. Again, very often such events were unlawful but went undetected or were not prosecuted.

Where such events involve the picking of a horse randomly, that is without any information upon which to base a judgment or guess, they amount to lotteries and the rules relating to lotteries apply – as set out above.

Otherwise, race nights are a form of betting and can only be conducted by a person with an operator's licence for betting. But, as can be seen in Chapter 7, all forms of commercial betting are prohibited in clubs and other premises with permission to sell or supply alcohol.

PART FOUR

HEARINGS AND APPEALS

9 Hearings

9.1 Introduction

Applications for club premises certificates or club gaming permits are heard, if a hearing is necessary, by a sub-committee of the local authority (licensing authority). Such hearings can vary from the well-organised court-like hearings, conducted in an atmosphere of professional calm, to disorganised public meetings.

The LA 2003 and the Gambling Act 2005 provide little guidance as to the nature and form of hearings before licensing authorities. Powers have been given to the Secretary of State to make regulations to govern such hearings. Otherwise, licensing authorities are at liberty to devise their own procedures.

Licensing authorities have no power to make orders for costs. The intention of the government was to limit the cost of making an application, thus reducing the burden on legitimate businesses, and also not to deter local residents from making appropriate representations.

Decisions will be made either by sub-committees or officers of the authority depending upon what matters have been delegated to those officers. In whichever circumstance, the 'common law' rules as to natural justice and the right to a fair hearing will continue to apply. Certainly wherever a decision of, say, a sub-committee has to be confirmed by the licensing authority, the final decision maker must be informed of the nature and effect of any representations made to the sub-committee and, in summary, the evidence put before the sub-committee.

Decision makers also have to have to the forefront of their minds the rights, often competing, contained in the European Convention on Human Rights as set out in the Human Rights Act 1998.

9.2 Rules and regulations

The Licensing Act 2003 (Hearings) Regulations 2005 (SI 2005/44) make provision for the procedure to be followed in relation to hearings held under the Act by the licensing authority. Detailed schedules contain time limits for holding of hearings (depending upon the nature of the application or matter to be determined), notices, documents to be provided with the notice of the hearing and the interpretation of the meaning of 'determination' as used in the Regulations.

The licensing authority must give notice of hearings, setting out the time date and place, to all parties in accordance with the provisions of LA 2003, Sch 2. The notice must be given no later than 10 working days before the hearing.

The notice of the hearing must be accompanied by information as to the rights of parties to attend, be represented and to take part in the hearing, the consequences of failure to attend, the procedure to be followed at the hearing and any particular points upon which the licensing authority will want clarification at the hearing from a party. In addition, the information set out in Sch 3 to the Regulations must also be provided to the relevant parties.

Upon receipt of a notice of hearing, a party must inform the licensing authority: (1) whether he intends to attend or be represented at the hearing; and (2) whether he considers a hearing to be necessary. That information is to be given by way of a notice. In addition, the notice must contain information as to witnesses whom the party wishes to call and details of the evidence they wish those persons to give as to the point or points upon which the witness may be able to assist the licensing authority.

The 'information' notice must be given to the licensing authority no later than 5 working days before the hearing.

9.3　Hearings

A licensing authority may dispense with a hearing if all parties agree and have given notice to that effect and if the authority so determines it must give notice to the parties that the hearing has been dispensed with.

If a party has told the authority that he does not intend to attend the hearing, then the hearing may proceed in his absence. If no such notice has been given but a party does not attend, the sub-committee dealing with the matter may either adjourn the hearing, where it considers it necessary in the public interest so to do, or may proceed in the party's absence to consider that party's application, representations or notice (as appropriate). If the authority determines to adjourn the hearing to a specified date it must, immediately, give notice to the parties of the new date, time and place of hearing.

Hearings have to be held within the time limits set out in Sch 1 to the Regulations and if a hearing is to be held on more than one day, it must be arranged to take place on consecutive working days. So that, for example, a hearing to determine an application for a premises licence must be held within 20 working days from the end of the period during which representations might be made. Unfortunately, to work out when that period ends one has to turn to the Licensing Act 2003 (Premises Licences and Club Premises Certificates) Regulations 2005 to discover that the relevant period is 28 consecutive days starting with the day after the day on which the application was given to the licensing authority by the applicant.

The licensing authority has the power to extend the time limits for a specified period where it considers that to be necessary in the public interest and may adjourn a hearing to a specified date or arrange for a hearing to be held on specified additional dates. Reasons must be given to the parties in the notice extending time limits, which has to be sent out immediately. There is no power to extend the period during which representations may be made. A party may withdraw any representation made by giving notice to the licensing authority no later than 24 hours before the first day of the hearing or orally at the hearing.

Hearings must usually be held in public. The licensing authority has the power to exclude members of the public, including parties and their representatives, from all or part of a hearing where it considers that the public interest in doing so outweighs the public interest in the hearing taking place in public. Any party to a matter may attend the hearing of that matter and be assisted or represented by any person whether or not that person is legally qualified.

9.4   Procedure

Subject to the Regulations it is for the licensing authority to devise its own procedure. The hearing is to take the form of a discussion led by the authority and cross-examination is not permitted unless the authority deems it necessary to enable it to consider the application, representations or notice (as appropriate). The procedure to be followed must be explained by the licensing sub-committee (licensing authority) to the parties at the beginning of the hearing. However, if a party has made an application, in his 'information' notice, for permission to call witnesses, that permission must not be withheld unreasonably.

Each party has the right to give further information, if clarification of any point or points has been sought (in the notice of hearing) by the licensing authority, in relation to such points; to question any other party, if given permission to so do; and to address the licensing sub-committee.

Members of the sub-committee may ask questions of any party or witness and may take account of documents or other information produced whether before the hearing or, with the consent of all the other parties, at the hearing.

Each party must be given an equal maximum period of time in which to exercise their rights to deal with points of clarification, question other parties and address the sub-committee. There is no provision in the regulations for the cross-examination by the parties of another party's witnesses. It is anticipated that, where appropriate, sub-committees will allow such cross-examination and that a licensing authority may provide for the exercise of that discretion within its own procedures.

A licensing sub-committee may require anyone disrupting a hearing to leave that hearing and may refuse to permit that person to return or allow him to return only on such conditions as they may specify. In the event of a person being excluded who could have provided information to the authority, the sub-committee must give that person the opportunity to put into writing what he had intended to say to the sub-committee.

A record of the hearing, in permanent and intelligible form must be kept by the authority for 6 years from the date of determination or the disposal of any appeal.

9.5   Decision making

The licensing sub-committee must disregard any information given by any party (or a witness called by that party) which is not relevant to either the application, representations or notice made by that party or the promotion of the licensing objectives.

The determination must be made within a period of 5 working days beginning with the last day of the hearing. Where a hearing has been dispensed with, the determination must be made within a period of 10 working days beginning with the day the authority gave notice to the parties that it had dispensed with the hearing.

Notification of any determination must be given in accordance with the particular provisions of the LA 2003 but where there is no specific provision within the Act then 'forthwith'. In all cases requiring notice of a decision to be given to the police where the police have not been a party to the hearing notice must be given immediately. Any notification of a determination to a party to the hearing must be accompanied by information as to the right of a party to appeal to the magistrates' court.

9.6   Irregularities

Failure to comply with the regulations before the licensing sub-committee makes its determination does not render the proceedings void. If anyone has been prejudiced by such a failure, the licensing authority must take such steps as it considers necessary to cure the irregularity before reaching its determination.

Clerical mistakes in any document recording a determination of a licensing authority arising from an accidental slip or omission may be corrected by the authority.

If not provided for in the regulations, rules as to debate, quorum, voting and other procedural matters relating to the functions of local authorities and local authority committees will be found in the local authority's standing orders. A copy of the standing orders is normally available for inspection by members of the public. It is normal practice for decisions to be taken by majority voting, with the chair having a second or casting vote.

9.7   Guidance

LA 2003, s 182 requires the Secretary of State to issue guidance ('the Guidance') to licensing authorities on the discharge of their functions under the LA 2003. The Secretary of State may revise the Guidance from time to time.

In carrying out its licensing functions, a licensing authority must have regard to any guidance issued by the Secretary of State under LA 2003, s 182. It must also have regard to its own licensing statement of policy made under LA 2003, s 5. Since, however, the making of the licensing statement is itself a licensing function, the authority must have regard to the Guidance when making that statement. In the Guidance, the Secretary of State has recognised that she cannot anticipate every possible scenario or set of circumstances that may arise and 'so long as the guidance has been properly and carefully understood and considered, licensing authorities may depart from it if they have reason to do so'. Licensing Authorities are cautioned, however, that if they do depart from the Guidance they will need to give full reasons for their actions.

With regard to hearings before a licensing authority, the guidance given is:

9.24   As a matter of practice, licensing authorities should seek to focus the hearing on the steps needed to promote the particular licensing objective which has given rise to the specific representation and avoid straying into undisputed areas. A responsible authority or interested party may choose to rely on their written representation. They may not add further representations to those disclosed to the applicant prior to the hearing, but they may expand upon their existing representation.

9.25   In determining the application with a view to promoting the licensing objectives in the overall interests of the local community, the licensing authority must give appropriate weight to:

- the steps that are necessary to promote the licensing objectives;

- the representations (including supporting information) presented by all parties;

- this Guidance; and

- its own statement of licensing policy.

Advice is given with regard to the imposition of conditions making it clear that conditions may only be imposed if necessary for the promotion of the licensing objectives. Conditions may not be merely aspirational but must be necessary for the promotion of the licensing objectives. Conditions relating to aspects covered by other legislation are deemed unnecessary and, therefore, could not be justified.

With regard to review hearings, the Guidance makes clear that licensing authorities may not initiate their own reviews. Those parts of the local authority identified as responsible authorities may, of course, initiate review proceedings but their representations must be treated in the same way as any other representations received by the licensing authority. The Secretary of State anticipates that responsible authorities and authorised persons will work together with licence holders and interested parties to meet the licensing objectives. Good practice will involve early warnings and advice when problems are identified.

Relevant parts of the Guidance published in October 2010 can be found in Appendix A3.

9.8   Representations by interested parties

Interested parties are defined as any of the following:

- a person living in the vicinity of the premises;

- a body representing persons who live in that vicinity;

- a person involved in a business in that vicinity;
- a body representing persons involved in such businesses;
- a member of the licensing authority.

Whenever interested parties oppose an application or seek a review of a premises licence or club premises certificate, there is first a filtering process involving a judgment as to whether or not the representation is relevant, that is, it is neither vexatious nor frivolous. The Guidance given by the Secretary of State is that it is a matter for the licensing authority to determine. The test is an objective one – whether an ordinary and reasonable person would consider the issues raised to be vexatious or frivolous.

'Vicinity' is not defined in the LA 2003. It is a matter to be determined in each case depending upon the circumstances of the case.

Licensing authorities must provide for a record to be taken of each hearing and kept in a permanent and intelligible form for 6 years from the date of determination or, following an appeal, the disposal of an appeal.

Whilst the Guidance expresses the hope that licensing authorities will place information about licensing applications, etc on their websites, there is no provision either in the Act or the Regulations for the public to be informed about the date, time and place of hearings.

10 Appeals

10.1 Introduction

Under the LA 2003 and the Gambling Act 2005, appeals lie from certain decisions of the licensing authority to the local magistrates' court. The former right of appeal from the magistrates' court to the Crown Court has been removed.

The supervisory role of the High Court through judicial review remains unaffected. The High Court, however, will continue to be reluctant to exercise its discretion where an alternative remedy exists. This means that, in most cases, a party aggrieved by a decision of a licensing authority in a particular case will be expected to seek a remedy in an appeal to the magistrates' court rather than challenge the authority through a claim for judicial review.

The LA 2003 and the Gambling Act 2005 do not make appeal decisions made by magistrates' courts 'final'. Whilst no appeal will lie to the Crown Court, the provisions relating to appeal by case stated will apply. The relevant statutory provisions are contained in Magistrates' Courts Act 1980, ss 111–114 and Magistrates' Courts Rules 1981 (SI 1981/ 552), rr 76–81. In addition, in relation to the proceedings before the High Court, CPR Pt 52 (Appeals) and the associated Practice Direction come into play. It is important to note that the time limit for making an application to the magistrates' court to state a case is inflexible. There is no power to extend the initial period of 21 days

The provisions relating to and, by omission, restricting rights of appeal from a decision of the licensing authority are to be found in LA 2003, s 181 and Sch 5 and in Gambling Act 2005, ss 206–209.

10.2 Powers of magistrates' courts

On an appeal against a decision of a licensing authority, a magistrates' court has a wide discretion. It may:

(1) dismiss the appeal;

(2) substitute for the decision appealed any other decision which could have been made by the licensing authority; or

(3)   restore a gaming permit (with effect from such date or on such transitional or other terms as the court may specify); or

(4)   remit the case to the licensing authority to dispose of it in accordance with the direction of the court; and

(5)   make an order as to costs.

An appeal to the magistrates' court will be by way of a rehearing. This means that different evidence may be presented and different submissions made. In particular, evidence of events occurring since the decision of the licensing authority was made will be admissible.

In *Sagnata Investments Ltd v Norwich Corporation* [1971] 2 QB 614 the Court of Appeal approved the judgments in the cases of *Stepney Borough Council v Joffe* [1949] 1 KB 599 and *R v Essex Quarter Sessions ex parte Thomas* [1966] 1 WLR 359 to the effect that, whilst the appeal court had to take into account the policy of the local authority, it was free to depart from it in appropriate circumstances.

The magistrates' court will be expected to give reasons for its decisions. This is now an expectation of all courts following the enactment of the Human Rights Act 1998. In particular, where in an appeal there are no objections and no evidence led against the appellant's case, cogent reasons would have to be given for reaching a conclusion adverse to the appellant. The reasons must be adequate. It is not sufficient to regurgitate the terms of the Act or to say that all the evidence and the submissions made have been considered. The parties should be able to ascertain from the statement of reasons why an application has been granted or refused.

10.3   Costs

On hearing an appeal, the magistrates' court also has a wide discretion as to costs. It may make such order as to costs as it thinks fit. The court must give its reasons for its decision as to costs. That discretion has been severely circumscribed by a line of authorities, which were reported in the first volume of *Licensing Law Reports*. Of particular importance are the decisions relating to the award of costs against local authorities and the police.

The conclusions to be drawn from those cases are:

•   in licensing cases, costs do not simply follow the event;

•   the provision to order such costs as the court thinks fit applies both to the quantum of the costs, if any, and as to which party should pay them;

- what the court will think just and reasonable will depend on all the relevant facts and circumstances of the case before the court;

- no order can be made against the police simply on the basis that costs follow the event. The court can only make such an order if it can be shown that the police's position has been unreasonable or prompted by some improper motive. If the police act responsibly in accordance with their duty under the LA 2003, no adverse order for costs can be made against them. It must be clear that the police have acted otherwise than in good faith or have acted unreasonably before they are exposed to an order for costs;

- where an appellant has successfully challenged an administrative decision made by the police or a regulatory authority acting honestly, reasonably, properly and on grounds that reasonably appeared to be sound, in the exercise of its public duty, the court should consider, in addition to any other relevant fact or circumstances, both:

  - the financial prejudice to the particular appellant in the particular circumstances if an order for costs is not made in his favour; and

  - the need to encourage public authorities to make and stand by honest, reasonable and apparently sound administrative decisions made in the public interest without fear of exposure to undue financial prejudice if the decision is successfully challenged.

10.4 Procedure

In general, an appeal lies to the magistrates' court for the petty sessions area in which the premises are situated. The appeal is commenced by giving notice of appeal to the justices' chief executive for the magistrates' court. Notice must be given within 21 days. The period of 21 days begins on the day on which the appellant was notified of the decision by the licensing authority.

If the police or an objector – that is a person who made relevant representations – is the appellant, then the holder of the club premises certificate or gaming permit becomes a respondent as well as the licensing authority.

Whereas when the applicant in relation to a premises licence or gaming permit is the appellant (in an appeal against a refusal to grant a premises licence, for example), those who opposed the grant (the police or local residents) are not made respondents. In those cases, the licensing authority has to bear the burden of presenting the case against grant to the magistrates' court. In exceptional circumstances and in order to carry out their functions under the relevant legislation, magistrates' courts may add parties to appeal proceedings.

10.5   Club premises certificate

LA 2003, Sch 5, Pt 2 provides a right of appeal where:

*   a licensing authority rejects an application for a club premises certificate or an application to vary the certificate;

*   a club certificate is granted, by the club against the imposition of conditions, or by an objector, who made relevant representations, against the grant or failure to impose appropriate conditions;

*   an application to vary the conditions of a club premises certificate is granted;

*   a decision has been made on an application for a review of a club premises certificate;

*   a club premises certificate is withdrawn by the licensing authority.

An appeal under LA 2003, Pt 2 must be made to the magistrates' court for the local justice area in which the premises concerned are situated. A notice of appeal must be given within 21 days to the justices' chief executive. The period of 21 days starts with the day on which the appellant was notified of the decision appealed against by the licensing authority.

Where the appeal is brought by an objector (a person who made relevant representations) then the club that holds or held the club premises certificate is made a respondent in addition to the licensing authority.

10.6   Club gaming permits and club machine permits

Gambling Act 2005, Sch 12, para 25 contains the appeal provisions in relation to Club Gaming Permits and Club Machine Permits. Paragraph 25 provides a right of appeal where:

*   a licensing authority rejects an application for the issue or renewal of a permit;

*   a licensing authority grants an application for the issue or renewal of a permit in relation to which objection was made;

*   a licensing authority cancels a permit;

- a licensing authority determines not to cancel a permit and a person made representations to the authority.

An appeal under the Gambling Act 2005 must be made to the magistrates' court for the local justice area in which the club's premises are situated by notice given to the designated officer within 21 days. The 21 days begins with the day on which the club or objector received the notice of the decision made by the licensing authority.

10.7 Temporary event notice

LA 2003, Sch 5, Pt 3, para 16 provides a right of appeal to the giver of a temporary event notice when a counter notice is served by the licensing authority following the lodging of a police objection. A similar right of appeal against a refusal to serve a counter notice is given to the police.

The provisions relating to the procedures and timetable are the same as with premises licences and club premises certificates, save that no appeal may be brought later than 5 working days before the day upon which the temporary event is due to start. Such a time limit is needed in order to give the magistrates' court time to arrange for the hearing of the appeal before the temporary event is due to take place.

There is no right of appeal against the service of a counter notice because the number of events promoted by the individual or in relation to the particular premises exceeds the statutory limits.

PART FIVE

INTERNAL REGULATION

11 Club Rules

11.1 Introduction

As mentioned earlier, clubs have been variously defined at law, but for the purposes of this chapter any definition must include a body of people with a sense of common purpose which is articulated through a set of rules. Outside the ambit of the LA 2003, the rules of the club still provide the foundation upon which all of the club's activities depend. Whether dealing with the use of club assets, the enrolment of new members or the settlement of disputes between members, the rules should cover any eventuality.

The rules that govern a club need not be 'legalese', or defy easy interpretation, but should articulate simply the ethos of the club and the manner in which its business is conducted. Invariably, they must include within their structure the objects of the club, and as will be seen below, they should allow the licensing authority to establish easily the bona fides of any application for a club premises certificate under the LA 2003. The rules must now also comply with the far-reaching provisions of the Equality Act 2010.

11.2 Minimum rules

As a generally suggested minimum, the rules should cover the following areas:

- purpose of the club;

- admission of members;

- management of the club's affairs/business;

- number and structure of committees;

- payment of fees/subscriptions;

- the removal of members;

- the holding of AGMs and other meetings;

- the making and amending of rules, byelaws and other forms of delegated authority.

Some rules are required by statute. Clubs that are affiliated to parent bodies or are registered as industrial, provident or friendly societies must also include any rules that are required under the legislation controlling registration. Thus, under Friendly Societies Act 1974, s 22(1)(b) and Industrial and Provident Societies Act 1965, s 14(1), the rules of such registered clubs are binding at law on the members (under both Acts the club is bound to provide a copy to a member on payment of a small sum). The rules of a club which is a limited company must reflect the requirements of the Companies Acts and its own memorandum and articles. Otherwise, the members of a club are free to determine the rules by which they wish their club to be run.

11.3   Contractual relationship

When a person agrees to join a club, the rules become binding on him or her. So long as a copy of the rules has been given to the prospective member or are available for inspection, or upon demand, they will be taken to be binding upon a member once he or she has paid a subscription. It is upon payment of the membership subscription that the contract is formed between the club and the member.

It follows that, should a paid up member be in breach of the rules, or fail to pay periodic subscriptions, then he or she is in breach of contract and may be expelled or penalised. This is not to say that the ruling of the club is the final word. As with any other contract, the interpretation of the rules is amenable to the scrutiny of the courts. The rules must be interpreted so as to be procedurally fair and compliant with natural justice.

Breaches of contract of this type would not usually come to the attention of the courts because they can be dealt with satisfactorily under the terms of the contract. The club rules are usually quite specific in relation to the consequences of a breach of them. The courts might be persuaded to intervene, however, if there is an allegation that the action taken by a club has resulted in some specific and quantifiable loss to the member, such as the loss of money or property. A member who believes that he has been expelled without justification, or wrongfully denied a specific right of membership, might persuade a court to intervene, but probably only if any rights of appeal under the rules have been exhausted. The rules might allow for an appeal to a specially appointed committee or panel of members, or they might allow for disputes over breaches of rules to be referred to independent arbitrators or mediators.

As was noted above, the rules should be easily interpreted and should not be deliberately technical or obscure. In the event of a dispute between the club and a member which does go to court, the court is unlikely to be persuaded by an overly technical reliance on the letter of the rules, where such an approach is likely to lead to manifest unfairness.

The general guidance in disputes of this nature is found in the words of Megarry V-C in the well-known case of *GKN Nuts & Bolts Ltd Sports and Social Club* [1982] 1 WLR 774 at 776:

> ... I think that the courts have to be ready to allow general concepts of reasonableness, fairness and common sense to be given more than their usual weight when confronted by claims to the contrary which appear to be based on any strict interpretation and rigid application of the letter of the rules. In other words, allowance must be made for some play in the joints.

11.4   Rules relating to qualification

If a club is to qualify for a premises certificate, its rules must make provisions in relation to applications for, and admission to, membership. The rules must provide that a person may not be admitted to membership, or to the privileges of membership, without an interval of at least 2 days between the date the person is nominated, or applies, for membership, and the date of admission to membership. In addition, the rules must make clear that where a person becomes a member without application or nomination, that person may not be admitted to the privileges of membership until at least 2 days after becoming a member. The rules should also make clear that when alcohol is supplied in the club's premises, such supply must be by or on behalf of the club. These requirements are dealt with in more detail in Chapter 2. Further, the club must have a membership of at least 25 and be established and conducted in good faith.

11.5   Good faith

LA 2003, s 63 concerns the licensing authority's decision on whether or not a club is conducted 'in good faith', that is, whether or not it is a genuine members' club – one that is run by the members for the benefit of the members, rather than one run for the benefit of an individual proprietor or proprietors. When making its decision, the licensing committee may consider, among other matters, the club's rules and arrangements concerning money, or other property of the club, or any gain that arises from carrying on the club. In particular, the licensing committee may take into account whether any such money, property or gain may be applied otherwise than for the benefit of the club as a whole, or for charitable, benevolent or political purposes.

The arrangements for giving members information about the finances of the club may also be taken into account. This is to enable the authority to satisfy itself that the members of the club retain control over the way in which it is managed and financed, and that they have access to the club's accounts.

The rules may also provide a useful vehicle for establishing that the additional conditions of qualification (those relating to the supply of alcohol) are also satisfied by the applicant club. Those conditions are set out in Chapter 3.

11.6   Management of club business

Whether on premises with the benefit of a club premises certificate, or elsewhere, the rules of the club are fundamental to the orderly management of club business. As stated above, it is imperative that the body of rules relied upon by the club is lucid, clear and comprehensive. It is human nature to challenge rules and much time is wasted where ambiguity allows differing interpretations of the rule. Invariably, plain language and a little foresight will serve the club well when rules are formulated or amended.

This chapter deals primarily with the requirements for unincorporated members' clubs. However, before proceeding to discuss these bodies it is worth recapping. A members' club may also be incorporated and limited by guarantee or shares, in which case the members from time to time form the company, and the rules of the club, which govern the conduct of members amongst themselves form part of either the memorandum or articles of association.

Other clubs may be unincorporated proprietary clubs, owned by an individual who is at liberty to set whatever rules he deems fit. These rules then become conditions of the contract which members enter to gain access. In consideration of the payment by the members of whatever fees the proprietor sets, the members or visitors are admitted to the club subject to the rules. However, in these clubs the proprietor is the final arbiter of the rules and of their implementation. Effectively, the same situation obtains in an incorporated proprietary club, where the company is the owner and it sets the rules.

Once the rules of the club have been drawn up, they should be faithfully adhered to. Disputes will be comparatively rare if it can be shown without doubt that actions taken are within the rules. Likewise, if the rules are clear, it should be obvious when something has been done in contravention of the rules.

Of greatest importance are the rules that control the conduct of club business, delegated authorities, voting rights and the discipline of members. There should be very clear rules as to what business is to be transacted by all the members in a general meeting, and what decisions may be delegated to elected committees or officers.

The manner in which general meetings of members and committee meeting are conducted tends to be a fruitful source of contention in members' clubs. When difficulties arise, it is usually because the rules of the club are not sufficiently clear or comprehensive. When the rules are being drawn up, some care should be taken to ensure that potential difficulties are anticipated and that rules are included to reduce the likelihood of their occurring, and to provide for resolving them when they do arise.

A template for club rules is set out in Appendix A1. Clubs that are affiliated to a parent society or association, such as the Club and Institute Union, usually adopt the model rules drawn up by the parent organisation. A basic example of the rules of a club can be found in Appendix A2.

11.7   Voting rights of members

The LA 2003 perversely omits any reference to a requirement in the rules for equal voting rights amongst members. Licensing Act 1964, Sch 8 dealt specifically with voting rights in clubs primarily for men or for women. It provided that in such clubs a rule that restricted voting to men or women, as the case may be, was not unlawful. There is nothing in the LA 2003 that renders clubs run primarily for men, or for women, ineligible for club premises certificates. At the time the LA 2003 was being drafted there had been a Private Members' Bill before Parliament (the Sex Discrimination (Clubs and Other Private Associations) Bill), which was intended to remove the common law exemption for private clubs and associations from the Sex Discrimination Act 1975 (and that under Licensing Act 1964, Sch 7). That Bill foundered. However, the Equality Act 2010, which came into force in October 2010, rendered such discrimination unlawful.

11.8   Equality Act 2010

Under Equality Act 2010, Pt 7, clubs are now required to ensure that there is no discrimination in the provision of access to goods and services or in the way that such 'associations' conduct their business.

Section 107 defines an 'association' as an association of persons: (1) which has at least 25 members; and (2) admission to membership of which is regulated by the association's rules and involves a process of selection. It matters not for the purposes of Pt 7 whether the association is incorporated or run for profit.

Section 107 gives a Minister of the Crown power to amend this definition so as to change the number of members required by the definition. It also provides that people who have any kind of membership of a particular association are protected by this Part, as are associates, who are not members of an association, but have many of the rights of members as a consequence of being a member of another association.

Part 7 makes any act of discrimination in respect of any of the relevant protected characteristics unlawful. The protected characteristics for Pt 7 are:

- disability;
- gender reassignment;
- pregnancy and maternity;
- race – this includes ethnic or national origins, colour and nationality;
- religion or belief;
- sex; and
- sexual orientation.

Under s 101 it is unlawful for a club or association to discriminate against, harass or victimise an existing or potential member, or an associate. Thus a club cannot refuse membership to a potential member or grant it on less favourable terms because of a protected characteristic. Associations can, however, restrict their membership to people who share a protected characteristic (Sch 16). A club cannot refuse an existing member or associate access to a benefit or deprive him or her of membership or rights as an associate because of a protected characteristic covered by Pt 7. This section is subject to s 103 (see below).

The statutory guidance gives the following examples of prohibited conduct under s 101:

- A gentlemen's club refuses to accept a man's application for membership or charges him a higher subscription rate because he is Muslim. This would be direct discrimination.

- A private members' golf club, which has members of both sexes, requires its female members to play only on certain days while allowing male members to play at all times. This would be direct discrimination.

Section 102 deals with the guests of members and makes it unlawful for a club to discriminate against, harass or victimise existing or potential guests. Specifically, a club cannot refuse to invite or admit a person as a guest because of a particular characteristic or invite that person on certain conditions which the association would not apply to other would-be guests. Equally, a guest cannot be refused access to a benefit simply because of a protected characteristic or subject to any other detriment. This is an extension of the disability rules to all relevant protected characteristics. This provision is subject to s 103.

Section 103 imposes a duty on a club or association to make reasonable adjustment for disabled members and guests (see below).

At s 103(2), the Act states that the provisions relating to harassment shall not apply in relation to the protected characteristics of: (1) religion or belief; (2) sexual orientation. The reason for this initially strange concession is that Sch 16 allows the clubs to restrict membership to those sharing a protected characteristic so long as access is not exclusively determined by reference to colour. It follows that whereas some people might be offended or excluded on the grounds of religion or sexual orientation, they are not permitted to raise a complaint in respect of harassment under the Act.

Schedule 16(1) states:

1 (1) An association does not contravene section 101(1) by restricting membership to persons who share a protected characteristic.

(2) An association that restricts membership to persons who share a protected characteristic does not breach section 101(3) by restricting the access by associates to a benefit, facility or service to such persons as share the characteristic.

(3) An association that restricts membership to persons who share a protected characteristic does not breach section 102(1) by inviting as guests, or by permitting to be invited as guests, only such persons as share the characteristic.

(4) Sub-paragraphs (1) to (3), so far as relating to race, do not apply in relation to colour.

(5) This paragraph does not apply to an association that is a registered political party.

If a club is in breach of the Act, members, guests, associates or applicants may seek recourse to the county court. Section 119 gives powers to county courts to grant any remedy that the High Court can grant in proceedings in tort or in a claim for judicial review. The remedies available are damages (including and not limited to compensation for injuries to feelings), an injunction and a declaratory relief. In cases based on indirect discrimination, if the respondent proves that he or she did not intend to treat the claimant unfavourably, then the award of damages cannot be considered until a court has looked at the other remedies available to it.

11.9   Changes to the rules

Club rules are not set in stone and may be amended when circumstances change. Maybe the aims and objects of the club have changed, or there has been a change of heart as to who may be admitted to membership.

It is vital that the club rules expressly permit change of the rules by the members. Societies registered under the Friendly Societies Act 1974 and the Industrial and Provident Societies Act 1965 are required under statute to make such provision. Those clubs falling outside statutory registration should, however, make such provision under their rules. Even where members have permitted the informal alteration of the rules or constitution of the club in the past, they are entitled to challenge any current change where it is imposed without provision in the rules for such a change. The reason for this is that as pointed out above the rules of the club effectively form the terms of the contract between the club and its members. When a member joins a club he or she does so on the basis of the rules then in force. Without the consent of one of the contracting parties the rules cannot be changed.

As a matter of good practice no rule change should be made retrospectively or retroactively, unless with the absolute concurrence of the membership (generally a specified majority). Where it is proposed that the rules be changed, then the resolution should be heard at the AGM or at a meeting of all members especially convened for that purpose.

If local authority licensing departments (licensing authorities) are to operate in an efficient and effective way it is important that their records are up to date. Consequently, LA 2003, s 82 imposes a duty on a club which holds a club premises certificate to give the licensing authority prompt notice of any changes to its rules. The licensing authority is then under a duty to amend its records accordingly.

The onus of complying with this statutory requirement is borne by the club secretary. When a club changes any of its rules, the secretary must give notice of the alteration(s) to the chief executive of the licensing authority within 28 days of the change being agreed. The notification must be accompanied by the club's premises certificate and the fee payable, currently £10.50.

If it is not possible to send the premises certificate to the licensing authority with the notification of rule change, the secretary must, instead, attach a statement of the reason for the failure to produce it. The local authority should be able to supply a copy of the premises certificate if it has been lost, stolen or mislaid (see para 3.12). It may charge a fee, currently £10.50, for supplying a copy document.

It is an offence for a club secretary to fail to give the required notice within the prescribed time limit. The penalty is a fine not exceeding £500.

Section 82 also imposes a duty on the club secretary to give notice to the local licensing authority of any change to the name of the club. The same procedures and penalties apply. The premises to which the club premises certificate relates cannot, though, be changed simply by giving notice under this section. Instead, the procedure for varying the premises to which the certificate relates, set out in Chapter 3, must be followed.

12 Officers and Trustees

12.1 Introduction

The officers and, where appropriate, trustees, of a members' club play an important part in the management and conduct of the club. The role played by particular officers may vary somewhat from club to club. In some clubs, all the officers may hold office in an honorary capacity. In others, the club's activities may be such that certain officers are paid to carry out their duties. Some of the officers, whether paid or unpaid, are liable in law for any breaches of statutory requirements that may occur at the club. A grasp of the general duties of the officers and trustees is essential if members' clubs are to be managed effectively and in accordance with the law.

12.2 The chairman/chair

The chairman or chair of a members' club has an important role. The chairman usually chairs general meetings of the members, and also the meetings of the management committee and, along with the other officers of the club, is responsible for seeing that the club is run smoothly and in accordance with the rules. It follows that the chairman must be fully familiar with all aspects of the club's rules and aims and objectives. The chairman should also be fully aware of any obligations, legal or otherwise, that the club may have.

Invariably, the chairman's is the most senior role in the club hierarchy, and he or she will often be consulted by the treasurer, secretary or steward in exercising their roles. Although the chairman, treasurer and secretary often carry out the day-to-day running of the club, the chairman enjoys perhaps a degree of seniority in his role and it is not uncommon for certain business or trading decisions to be taken by him or her where expediency demands action. This does not mean that the chairman enjoys presidential powers, but simply that he or she will generally have sufficient experience and knowledge of club policy and procedures to exercise a discretion that can be ratified by the management committee.

Along with the club secretary, it is the chairman who is liable to prosecution if the licensing laws are broken by the club, but the chairman is not usually personally liable for the club's debts unless the chairman has entered into a contract on behalf of the club that was not authorised by the club. The chairman is often the public face of the club and so should behave in a manner that is above reproach at all times.

Arguably, the most important responsibility the chairman has is in relation to general meetings of members. It is the chairman who is responsible for the proper conduct of the meeting, and so should have confidence and an air of authority that will ensure that discussions take place in an orderly, sensible fashion and in accordance with the rules of the club and the provisions of licensing legislation. As is stated above, the chairman must exercise his function at meetings with care and fairness.

12.3   The secretary

The club secretary is responsible for ensuring that the instructions of the committee in relation to the every-day running of the club are carried out. The secretary should ensure that important club documents and authorisations are kept safely, and maintain proper club records of, for example, members' names and addresses. It is the secretary's role to ensure that subscriptions are paid and that certain payments from the club are met, such as premises insurance, VAT returns and Performing Right Society licensing renewals. Although the role of secretary is invariably honorary (unpaid!) it is recognised as an onerous task, attracting sanction if certain of his statutory functions are not discharged.

The secretary has certain duties under the LA 2003. The secretary must ensure that the licensing authority is notified of any change of name and of any alteration to the club rules (s 82(6)). The secretary should also take responsibility for giving notice of any change of relevant registered address for the club (s 83(6)). Most importantly, the club secretary is responsible for ensuring that the club's premises certificate is kept under the control of a nominated person and that a summary of it is prominently displayed on the club's premises, along with a notice specifying the position held by the nominated person (s 94(5)). Similarly, the secretary is charged with the requirement to produce the club premises certificate for amendment within 14 days of request by the licensing authority (s 93(3)). The secretary commits an offence if these functions are not met, and although the fine is only a level two fine (£500) it is a mark of the responsibility of this post that this officer is specifically identified in the LA 2003 as the responsible person.

12.4   The treasurer

The Licensing Act 1964 contained a provision that a club should be considered to be conducted in good faith only if it had satisfactory arrangements for giving members proper information about the finances of the club, and allowed them access to the books of account and other records kept, to enable them to ensure the accuracy of that information.

These provisions were replicated and expanded in the LA 2003. Section 63 states that, in considering whether a club is established and conducted in good faith as a members' club, account is to be taken, among other matters, of:

• any provision in the rules or arrangements under which money or property of the club, or any gain from carrying on the club, is or may be applied otherwise than for the benefit of the club as a whole or for charitable, benevolent or political purposes;

• the arrangements for giving members information about the finances of the club; and

• the books of account and other records kept to ensure the accuracy of that information.

Generally, it is the members of a club who elect a treasurer and appoint an auditor or auditors to oversee the accounts. These elections and appointments should be made at the AGM and notice of them should be given as items for determination by the members. In many clubs the position of club treasurer may be purely honorary, but in large clubs a salary or stipend may be paid.

The office of treasurer is not one that should be taken on without mature consideration. Some statutory duties do have to be shouldered by the treasurer. For example, the treasurer is responsible for ensuring that the club complies with tax laws. The duties may include dealing with salaries, income tax and capital gains tax as well as the payment of invoices and accounts tendered to the club for payment. The treasurer will be responsible for banking membership fees and keeping proper accounts in relation to them. The treasurer is also responsible for the conduct of the club's banking business.

The treasurer does not, however, carry out these duties independently. The management committee gives directions with regard to financial transactions, the treasurer making such payments as are directed and generally dealing with funds in accordance with the wishes of the committee. In certain circumstances, financial matters may be referred to the members in general meeting. The treasurer is bound to act on any decisions the members take in respect of those matters.

Generally, the treasurer has no personal liability for the debts of the club, but may become liable for acts outside the instructions given or by acting in excess of delegated authority. For example, if the treasurer were to enter into a contract for the supply of goods that was not authorised by the members or the management committee, the treasurer could be held personally liable for the debt to the supplier.

12.5 Trustees

A members' club does not have to have trustees to be a qualifying club for the purposes of the LA 2003. However, trustees may be appointed if there is a need for club property or assets to be held in trust by a group of trustees who will take care of the property or assets on behalf of the members (indeed it is a statutory duty under the Friendly Societies Act 1974 for all working men's clubs to appoint one or more trustees (Friendly Societies Act 1974, s 24) and for the resolution appointing a trustee to be filed with the Financial Services Authority (s 24(3)).

Unincorporated associations are unable to hold property in the name of the club. (It is impossible for land to be registered for instance by an unincorporated association as it has no legal personality.) Named individuals must hold the property on behalf of the club, and they must hold it on trust for the benefit of all the members. Members' clubs that are incorporated, such as those that are limited companies or associations registered as provident or industrial societies, are able to hold property in their corporate names, and so do not need trustees to hold property on the members' behalf.

In general terms, the duty of trustees is to hold property on trust for the members of the club. Trustees are not usually expected to play any part in the management of the club, although they are bound to carry out any instructions they are given in relation to the club's property by the management committee, which should be articulating the wishes of the membership. They do, however, have a duty to make sure that the property is preserved and its value is maintained by ensuring that assets are used properly and not put at risk by improper or reckless action taken by those who manage the club's affairs. This is sometimes a difficult concept where trustees are viewed as acting at the bidding of the committee. Nevertheless, the trustee acts upon his or her own cognizance to ensure that the assets in his or her trust are neither dissipated nor wasted; this is again a personal and onerous responsibility which should not be lightly entered into, not least because the trustee has no right to be indemnified by individual club members in the event that he suffers a loss in the discharge of his duties (unless the rules expressly so provide (*Wise v Perpetual Trustee Co* [1903] AC 139). However, a trustee of a club does have a personal lien over the trust property vested in him, to cover any liabilities incurred by him on the club's behalf.

The precise nature of the trustees' responsibilities may be determined by reference to a number of sources. First, there is the deed of trust drawn up when the trust was set up. That document should contain details of the trustees' duties, powers and responsibilities in relation to the trust property. The trustees are bound by that deed and expected to comply with it at all times.

Next, the general law of trusts is of relevance. This body of law is wide and complex. Even so, the trustees must comply with it, and are liable to a civil action for breach of trust if they contravene it.

The rules of the club may also be relevant. In many instances, the rules make specific provision for the appointment of trustees; their term of office; how they may be replaced; and the rights they have, if any, to attend meetings and to vote on resolutions put before the members. If they are members as well as trustees, they are enfranchised. They may also be given the right to attend committee meetings, although they are not likely to be able to vote on matters being decided by the committee since they have not been elected as members of it.

Finally, in the case of clubs affiliated to a parent organisation, such as the Royal British Legion or a political association, the trustees may be expected to comply with national guidelines. The adoption of model rules in relation to trustees has obvious advantages. The club can be reasonably sure that the national guidelines have been fully considered and deal with all the important issues in relation to trustees. In addition, by adopting a national model, the management committee is relieved of the onerous task of drafting rules that adequately cover all aspects of the subject.

As a general rule, trustees do not have any personal liability in relation to the debts incurred by the club. Nor are they liable for any compensation or damages that may be ordered in respect of actions brought against the club. Trustees should be aware, however, that should it be found that the members of the club have suffered a financial loss as a result of negligence on their part or failure by them to carry out their duties as trustees, they could be sued for breach of trust and ordered to compensate the members.

Trustees should generally be protected by the club for which they hold property (whether leasehold or freehold) by the devising of terms limiting their personal liability to the extent of the club's assets. Of course the easiest way of avoiding what is increasingly seen as a burdensome role is to consider incorporating the club. Once incorporated, the club takes on its own legal personality and can hold property and assets in its own right.

What follows is a brief consideration of the forms of liability which may attend the committee's/trustees' running of the club.

12.6   The commercial relationship between unincorporated associations with other parties

As has been noted, those clubs which are unincorporated have no free-standing legal identity of their own. Thus the formation of legal relations with third parties such as suppliers and tradesmen is problematic and tends to fall back on the personal capacity of whoever has been chosen to represent the club.

The trustees and committee of a club only have the capacity to contract on behalf of members, which has been granted under the rules or arises by reasonable implication. They have only the authority vested in them by the constitution. It is ordinarily the case that the trustees or committee cannot pledge the credit of members, as a class, and nor can they pledge the credit of other committee members.

There are very good reasons why the authority given to the committee to trade or contract, arising under the rules, expressly or impliedly, should not bind members. Not least of these is that members are only liable under the constitution to pay an annual subscription – they are not shareholders.

Ordinarily, a committee will only undertake to purchase that which it can afford with the club's available funds. Thus clubs often have a bar and bar account on which stock is purchased for onward sale. The goods are paid for from their re-sale and the money accrues to the trading account. If all goes well, there should be no question of demand being made by creditors, as the brewery is paid on a monthly basis. If the goods are consumed by the members, but as a result of poor business practice the brewery's credit is abused, the committee could seek to raise a special subscription. If the members declined to pay a further subscription they would not be individually liable for the shortfall.

Where, however, the club has authorised an officer to obtain credit, but is specifically in control of the funds (rather than delegating responsibility to one of the officers), then the members may well be liable (*Cockerell v Aucompte* (1) 2 C B (NS) 440 – secretary authorised to purchase goods but not in control of the funds to do so – impliedly required to obtain credit).

In the case of employment, of course, there are far greater contingent liabilities arising from the contract of employment and where the committee is authorised to employ staff, the members are jointly liable for the performance of the contract.

12.6.1 What is the scope of the committee's authority?

If the rules clearly encompass the actions of the committee in entering into a contract or obtaining a line of credit, purchasing goods, etc, then the members may well be liable under the liabilities flowing from those transactions. By the same token, if the committee enters into a contract which is subsequently ratified by the members then they accept liability for that contract, although ordinarily only up to the value of their individual subscriptions.

Where an officer enters into a contract which is obviously outside the authority of the club, the members are not bound by it.

The law of agency is complex and the scope of this chapter does not allow for a fuller discussion. Clubs should obtain legal advice before entering into substantial commercial arrangements or considering the extent of committee authority to conduct the club's business.

12.6.2 Liability of the officers and trustees

Ordinarily, whilst individual officers have contracted on a credit basis with the consent or acquiescence of the members they are not individually liable for a default. Nevertheless, as has been already noted in relation to trustees, the potential outcome can be personally ruinous and clubs should make efforts to protect the officers who take on responsibility for contracts:

- if the other party will agree, personal liability of a committee member may be capped at the limit of the club's funds. Plainly, the third party is under no obligation to accept such a term;

- the committee may raise subscriptions or levy a one-off payment;

- the committee may assert a lien over the assets of the club in respect of liabilities arising from authorised activity;

- the committee may be offered a limited form of indemnity in case of legal action arising from authorised activity.

13 Meetings

13.1 Introduction

In this chapter, some of the common day-to-day problems that arise when transacting club business are considered. The rules should deal with the calling of meetings and the conduct of business at those meetings, whether they be annual or extraordinary meetings of the club members, or committee meetings where delegated powers are exercised for the efficient running of the club. Members' clubs cannot always afford to employ full-time professional officers experienced in the conduct of formal business meetings, and as most business is conducted by volunteers the conduct of these meetings is often not expert, and can give rise to disputes.

This chapter seeks to highlight best practice for the convening and conduct of meetings. Often, clubs affiliated to national organisations or to the Club and Institute Union may find that they are expected to follow specific procedures set out in a manual provided by the organisation. The guidance given in this chapter will be of greatest benefit to those clubs that have no such allegiance.

13.2 Old clubs

Problems may arise in relation to the conduct of a general meeting of members as a result of an omission from the LA 2003. Whether by accident, oversight or design, certain statutory provisions that had been an important part of the legislation relating to members' clubs were not repeated in the new Act. For reasons unknown, the LA 2003 failed to replicate the requirements for the internal governance of clubs found in the Licensing Act 1964.

Licensing Act 1964, Sch 7 made provisions in relation to club rules. That schedule imposed obligations on registered clubs in relation to:

- the management of the club;

- general meetings;

- membership; and

- elective committees.

In relation to general meetings, the Schedule provided:

- that there must be a general meeting of the club at least once a year and that there must not be more than 15 months between general meetings;

- that both the general committee and the members must be capable of summoning meetings;

- that general meetings must be confined to members;

- that all members entitled to use the club premises must be entitled to vote and have equal voting rights (no casting vote for the chairman); and

- for exceptions to the general rules in relation to voting rights in certain specified circumstances.

The exceptions concerning voting rights may be summarised as follows:

- there may be a rule that excludes from voting members under a certain age; if the club is primarily for former members of Her Majesty's Forces, persons who have not been in the services may be excluded from voting (By reason of Equality Act 2010, Sch 16, these provisions became unlawful in October 2010.);

- if club rules provide for family membership or family subscriptions, persons who use the club by virtue of being a member of a family but who are not themselves members may be excluded from voting.

The Schedule also required clubs to have at least one elective committee. An elective committee must consist of members of the club, elected each year at a general meeting for a period of not less than 12 months and not more than 5 years. Elections have to be held annually and, if all the elected members are not to go out of office each year, the rules must make clear which of them are to go out of office each year. The Schedule allowed for casual vacancies to be filled by appointment.

Elective committees are expected to deal with all matters that are not reserved for decision by the members in general meeting. It follows that the rules of a members' club should spell out which matters are to be decided by the members and which may be delegated to elective committees or to club officers.

The Licensing Act 1964 did not contain any requirements as to the election of officers. It is left for the members to decide whether the officers of the club should be elected by the members in general meeting or whether, having elected a committee to manage the club's day-to-day affairs, it should be left to that committee to elect its own chairman and secretary. Typically, the members of a club elect a club chairman, club secretary and honorary treasurer, and those officers become ex officio members of the elective committee.

A club registered under the Licensing Act 1964 is bound by the provisions of Sch 7 if it was granted a premises certificate under the transitional provisions for the LA 2003. This is because, although the Licensing Act 1964 was repealed completely upon the coming into full force of the LA 2003, the new certificate is granted subject to conditions which reproduce the effect of any restriction imposed on the use of the premises for the existing qualifying club activities. Regulations made pursuant to the LA 2003 make clear that the Licensing Act 1964 falls within this provision. As a consequence, existing members' clubs continue to be required to comply with the requirements in relation to general meetings set out in the Licensing Act 1964.

13.3   New clubs

Potential difficulties arise in relation to clubs that obtain premises certificates under the provisions of LA 2003, Pt 4. Where no representations are made in relation to an application, the licensing authority may impose only such conditions as are consistent with the club operating schedule, and the mandatory conditions set out in ss 73 (concerning off-sales), 74 (concerning the showing of films on club premises) and 74A (mandatory conditions relating to the sale or supply of alcohol) of the Act. Even where representations have been made, the licensing authority is authorised to impose only such additional conditions as are necessary for the promotion of the licensing objectives.

Even if licensing authorities appreciate the potential difficulties resulting from the failure to provide statutory controls over the conduct of club meetings, it is unlikely that they will be able to assist by imposing conditions similar to those contained in Licensing Act 1964, Sch 7, described above, since it is difficult to see how such conditions could be said to be necessary for the promotion of the licensing objectives.

If a new club is free from the constraints of the Licensing Act 1964, there is a risk that its affairs may fall into the hands of a minority who may seek to run it in a way that does not meet the wishes of the majority. In such circumstances there is a possibility that the club is not being operated in good faith and members need to ensure that the wishes of the majority are reflected in club governance. It is still arguably best practice to voluntarily adopt a model of governance based on Licensing Act 1964, Sch 7, although the Act has been repealed.

13.4   Delegated powers

Whatever the statutory position, the health and well-being of a members' club depends on its affairs being conducted in a regular and transparent fashion, and in the best interests of the members generally. Problems can arise when attempts are made to run a members' club otherwise than in accordance with recognised business procedures. Club rules can be used to prescribe the procedures to be followed. If so, each rule must be set out in simple, clear, unequivocal language to keep any disputes to a minimum.

When a decision needs to be made in relation to the running of a members' club, it is necessary to consider first whether the matter must be referred to the members as a whole, or whether the officers or a club committee can deal with the matter under delegated powers. Generally, proposals for changes to the constitution of a club, or to its principal objectives or rules, should be put before all the members for decision. Matters relating to the day-to-day running of the club, such as the employment of staff, the ordering of stock and services and the maintenance of order and discipline, are probably best dealt with by the committee or an officer. It is vital that the club rules specify which matters must be decided by all the members, and which are to be delegated.

The manner in which delegated powers are to be exercised may also need to be spelt out in the rules. For example, where an officer or committee has the authority to conduct proceedings in relation to allegations of indiscipline, the rules should specify how those proceedings should be conducted and what rights the member has at the disciplinary hearing. Difficulties may arise if these matters are not clearly defined in the rules. A decision taken by committee should be the fair product of quorate meeting and the executive action or decision of an officer should be specified by the rules. Members should never lose sight of the fact that officers with the delegated power to act on their behalf make executive decisions that are binding on them. Similarly, if a club committee has power to take a decision, it binds the members.

By the same token, officers and committees need to ensure that they act at all times in the best interest of the members, avoiding conflicts of interest or any allegation that they have benefited by their actions.

Sometimes, where a committee or officer clearly has the delegated authority to deal with a particular issue but chooses not to because of the complex or grave nature of the problem, a general meeting of members must be called. A resolution should be drawn up and publicised, and the members should be asked to vote on that resolution and any amendments that may be submitted.

13.4.1 Terms of reference

Licensing legislation has never contained provisions regulating the manner in which the general decision-making processes in members' clubs should be delegated or the way in which officers or elected committees should reach their decisions or conduct their business. It has always been left to the members to decide issues of delegation, and the decisions reached by them in that regard should be enshrined in the club's rules.

The matters that should be delegated, and to whom, are often self-evident, the decisions being driven by practical considerations. For example, it would be wholly impracticable for all the members to have to make day-to-day decisions affecting the running of the club's affairs or to negotiate contracts with suppliers and others doing work for the benefit of members. The members as a whole could not be actively concerned in the recruitment and interviewing of staff, although the number of staff to be employed and the level of wages to be paid may be matters to be agreed in general meeting. Again, when disciplinary action against an individual member needs to be taken it would not, as a general rule, be practicable for the members to be involved, even though decisions about the sort of behaviour that might lead to disciplinary action might be agreed by the members generally.

It is important that club rules deal, in unambiguous terms, with who is authorised to deal with what, and the basis upon which delegated powers are to be exercised. For the avoidance of doubt, the rules may also be used as a vehicle for ensuring that club committees are run on proper, business-like lines and that all those entitled to participate in decisions are able to do so.

One function of the delegated authority of the committee is the framing of bye laws, which by their nature should be wholly subordinate to the rules. Bye laws can only be made by express authority of the club rules and should be aimed at the better management of club business. Bye laws are not intended to be, nor should they be, set up in opposition to the rules and ethos of the club. The rule that enables the making of bye laws should set out the procedural scope of bye laws, and the members should be advised of any such rule by advertising it on the club notice-board, or for that matter by letter or email to the members. Some constitutions may prefer the passing of bye laws at a general meeting, although they are still framed by the committee. (The issue of bye laws belongs in this chapter because it is a function of the delegated authority of the committee.)

13.5 General meetings

13.5.1 Convening a general meeting

Club rules must as a matter of basic governance include rules for the calling of general meetings and those rules should be adhered to. In the interests of minimising disagreement about procedures, clubs should take into account the statutory requirements set out at the beginning of this chapter. Every member who is entitled to attend a general meeting and to vote on issues raised for discussion should be given reasonable notice of the date and time of the meeting and the venue for it. The notice should give full details of the matters to be discussed and the decisions to be made. Any decision taken without proper notice being given to members is open to challenge by one of the methods described below. The club rules should make clear what is to be regarded as reasonable notice. It is suggested that, in the absence of emergency, a minimum of 7 days' notice should be given. If the rules of the club do not indicate the manner in which notice is to be given, it is within the recognised competence of the committee to decide how such notice is to be given (*Labouchere v Earl of Wharncliffe* (1879) 13 ChD 346).

Sometimes difficulties arise because attempts are made during general meetings to deal with matters that were not canvassed in the notice convening the meeting. The temptation to do so should be resisted. This is because a member who has chosen not to attend the meeting on the basis of the information given in the convening notice may, justifiably, complain that he would have attended and taken part had he known the other issue was to be determined. The conduct of all meetings should observe the rules and the rules must be applied in accordance with natural justice.

It is strongly recommended that the general provisions contained in Licensing Act 1964, Sch 7 be incorporated in club rules and adhered to. Such rules would then fix the frequency with which general meetings are to be held; establish the basis upon which extraordinary meetings may be called; and provide that at general meetings of the club, every member who is entitled to vote is allowed to do so and every member, including the person chairing the meeting, is to have an equal vote. The chairman should not have a casting vote at general meetings.

13.6 Voting

Recognised business practice requires that any proposition or resolution that is put before the members must have the support of more than 50% of the voting members if it is to be adopted. If there is a tie, or if fewer than 50% of the voting members give their support to the resolution, it should be declared to have been lost.

Amendments to any resolution that is put before the members should be allowed. Where an amendment is tabled, it should be voted upon first. If more than 50% of the voting members support the amendment, it is agreed and the original resolution should be declared to have been lost. If the amendment fails to gain the required support, it should be declared to have been lost and the original resolution should then be put to the vote.

If several amendments have been tabled they should be voted upon in turn, until such time as one of them receives the support of more than 50% of the voting members. At that point the successful amendment should be declared adopted and the original resolution should not be put to a vote. If all amendments fail to receive the required support, a vote should be taken on the original resolution. At all times the chairman should ensure that the meeting is conducted in good order. If the meeting degenerates into disorder, then the chairman may adjourn the meeting, but only for so long as required for the efficient conduct of the club's business, and never to procrastinate.

Minutes should be taken of the matters raised and the decisions reached at the general meeting, and the club rules should provide for the proper dissemination of those minutes to members.

13.7 Committee meetings

13.7.1 Convening a committee meeting

Elected members of any committee should be given proper notice of the dates and times of meetings. Generally, the business at such meetings should follow a published agenda, although it might be agreed in urgent cases that a matter be discussed and determined even though it was not mentioned in the agenda. It is not usually necessary for the committee secretary to send each committee member formal notice of each meeting. Meetings may be scheduled on a fixed basis, for example, on the third Wednesday in each month, or the dates of meetings might be fixed in advance for a period of, say, 12 months. Each committee member would then be responsible for being present at committee meetings, and the secretary would give notice only of any changes to the published arrangements.

13.7.2 The conduct of meetings

The rules should specify a quorum for any committee meeting, and that business should not be transacted if the required number of members is not present at the meeting. In the latter circumstances, the meeting should be postponed until the minimum number of members is able to attend. Business transacted in the absence of the necessary quorum is void.

A person should be elected to chair committee meetings, and a person should be nominated or elected to take a note of the matters raised and the decisions taken. All members should be entitled to see the minutes taken at committee meetings, so it is important that the matters discussed and the decisions taken are properly recorded.

Difficulties often arise in relation to the keeping and publishing of committee minutes. It is often argued that if minutes have to be made available to all the members, free and frank discussion of agenda items may be inhibited. Matters relating to the conduct or discipline of members tend to give rise to the greatest degree of concern. Committee members frequently argue that they could not be completely open about their views if their comments must then be made available to any member who may wish to see them. This difficulty usually arises because of a misunderstanding about the nature of minutes. Minutes need be only a brief summary of the proceedings at a meeting. They should not take the form of a verbatim account of the discussions. They should set out each of the items raised for discussion and/or decision and record the decisions reached as a result. Minutes should not contain the detail of the discussions that gave rise to the decisions reached. If the correct style is used for minutes and the detailed discussions are regarded as confidential to committee members, the members can be kept in touch with the decisions being made on their behalf while minimising the risk of bad feeling.

The statutory requirements in relation to voting that apply in the case of general meetings of the club (see above) do not apply to committee meetings. Specifically, while good practice demands that every member of a committee should have a vote whenever a decision is to be made, the person chairing the meeting can be given a casting vote in the interests of ensuring that progress is made in all discussions and to avoid stalemate situations. If the rules for committee meetings allow it, the person in the chair can resolve any stalemate by recording a casting vote.

A question which sometimes arises is whether a member of a committee may abstain from voting on a particular proposition. The answer is that committee members are not compelled to cast a vote, any more than a person is compelled to vote in local or national elections. If, though, a committee member were to make a practice of abstaining, the broader issue of whether that person should remain a member of the committee may arise. If a member rarely contributes to the decision-making process that person's worth as a member of the committee may well be open to question.

When the result of a ballot is being determined, abstentions should be recorded and taken into account. In some cases an abstention may have the effect of a vote against the motion, since it may result in a failure to achieve a majority in support. Without majority support any motion is of course lost.

13.7.3 Maintaining committees

Ordinarily, the composition of a club committee should be determined by the members of the club and set out in the club's rules. The persons to serve on it are elected at the annual general meeting. The rules should specify the period during which each elected committee member should hold office. Typically, the rules provide for a system of retirement by rotation, with retiring members being eligible for re-election should they wish to be considered for a further period in office. It is quite common to find that, initially, some members are elected for 3 years, some for 2 years and some for one year. The number of votes cast determines who is elected for which period of time, those with the highest number being elected for the longest period and those with the smallest vote serving for the shortest term.

The numbers serving on a committee may be reduced: a member may find that other commitments make it impossible to continue to serve; a member may move away from the area; or there may be a death or incapacity that gives rise to a depletion of committee numbers. It is prudent for clubs to anticipate such eventualities and to make provision in the rules for filling casual vacancies. Some clubs may prefer to call an extraordinary general meeting and hold an election to find a replacement member. Others may be content to give the committee authority to co-opt a member onto the committee to fill the vacancy until the next scheduled elections are held.

13.8   The election of officers

In some clubs, the officers elected by the members in a general meeting automatically serve on the club's management committee. On the other hand, the affairs of a club may be entrusted to a number of committees rather than a single management committee. For example, a club may have a 'bar committee' which oversees the supply of alcohol to members and guests, and an 'entertainments committee' which takes responsibility for engaging entertainers and organising functions. In such cases there are no statutory controls in relation to the election of officers. Ordinarily, it is for the members of each committee to elect one of their colleagues to take the chair at meetings and another to act as secretary. The rules should make clear whether committees have the delegated authority to take such decisions.

13.9   Duty to act fairly

At all levels of the meeting and decision-making process the members, committee and officers must conduct business fairly. This level of fairness should be evident from the rules; thus AGMs should be a fixed part of the club diary. The rules should ensure that adequate notice is given to the members and that the agenda is circulated in advance. The quorum for AGMs and committee meetings should be set by the rules and in either event an agenda should be circulated. Again, registered clubs are generally in a far better position than 'new' clubs to ensure such fairness.

13.10   Challenges by members

If difficulties do arise once a club premises certificate has been obtained, perhaps because of the absence of democratic management, there may be several courses open to aggrieved members. One possibility is that they may be able to convince the licensing authority that there are grounds for a review of the relevant premises certificate. Such a course of action would, however, succeed only if the authority is satisfied that the grounds for the application are relevant to one or more of the licensing objectives contained in s 4(2) – the prevention of crime and disorder; public safety; the prevention of public nuisance; or the protection of children from harm. Otherwise, the application for review would be rejected.

Another possibility is that a sufficient number of members may be prepared to support a vote of no confidence in the officers and/or the management committee. It is arguable, however, that the elected committee would not be bound to act upon such a resolution and arrange for new elections to be held unless the rules of the club specifically allowed for the removal of officers or committees on the basis of a motion of no confidence. The argument is that without such a provision in club rules, any decision that officers or committee members be removed from office would be ultra vires.

Another approach that dissatisfied members may be able to take is to question whether their club is being conducted in good faith. A members' club must be established and conducted in good faith if it is to be regarded as a qualifying club (see Chapter 3). This course of action would require members to contact the licensing authority to suggest that their club no longer qualifies for a club premises certificate since it is no longer established and conducted in good faith. If the licensing authority is satisfied that the allegation is true, it has the power to withdraw the premises certificate in accordance with LA 2003, s 90. If necessary, the licensing authority may call upon the police, persuading them to apply to the magistrates for a warrant to enter the club premises and search them for evidence in support of the allegation that the club is no longer established and run in good faith. The disadvantage of this course of action would be that, if it is successful, the club's premises certificate would be withdrawn. A new application for a club premises certificate would have to be made if the members wished to continue to operate as a members' club, and it would then be for the members to convince the licensing authority that the club now qualified for a certificate in that it is again established and conducted in good faith.

14 Conduct of Members and Guests

14.1 Introduction

Whatever the purpose of a club, be it special interests, sport or social, people will fall out occasionally. Sometimes guests misbehave in bars, or do not give way to the club captain on the 9th hole, attracting opprobrium on the member who invited them. On other occasions members fall out over the use of club facilities (for instance the shooting of a flight pond, or misusing property kept by a model aeroplane club!). Very often, members do not fall out over such esoteric disputes as the examples drawn above (both from experience). They may often simply get drunk and behave badly at the bar, or persist in minor breaches of the rule simply to prove a point. This chapter examines the ways in which disputes may arise within a club and the best way in which they should be handled

14.2 The duty of members and guests

Members and their guests are expected to behave as well on club premises as they would anywhere else in public. Where members or guests are using club facilities, they are expected to obey the rules of the club and not to behave in a way which causes nuisance or annoyance to any other members. By the same token anyone on club premises is required to obey the law as he or she would anywhere else. Thus, criminal behaviour such a selling illicit goods (EU tobacco, counterfeit goods, etc), which is often regarded as 'harmless' but may result in the loss of the club premises certificate, cannot be tolerated.

Where by his or her behaviour a member breaks the law or commits a serious misdemeanour, the club rules must allow for review and sanction of that behaviour. Similarly, the rules should allow for occasions where the guest of a member behaves badly.

The rules, when they are drafted, should be as clear and unambiguous on points of discipline and sanction as on other points. Remembering that the rules form the terms of the contract between the club and members is vital when the disciplinary provisions are decided. If a particular sanction such as expulsion or suspension is not a present term of the rules it cannot be used to deal with breaches of the rules (without going to the extraordinary lengths of changing the rules retrospectively, which would then be a breach of natural justice – see below). The members should decide, in a general meeting, the broad standards of behaviour they expect of members and guests, and their expectations should be set out in the rules. It may be appropriate to set out specific acts or types of conduct that are not allowed on club premises.

14.3   Penalties for misconduct

The penalties for misconduct may include:

*   suspension;

*   expulsion;

*   a fine;

*   match bans or suspensions from sporting or competition events.

A fine is generally not an option because of the difficulty of arriving at the appropriate penalty for the misconduct in question, and the even greater problem of enforcing payment. (What powers of recovery does the club have, other than the threat of expulsion?)

Within many sporting clubs there may also be a disciplinary function relating to misconduct, for instance on the field of play. The sanctions available in these circumstances are less likely to be as blunt as suspension or expulsion, and may involve a match ban, or other disciplinary measure. It follows nevertheless that a player may engage in such an egregious display of violence or misconduct on the pitch that he or she falls to be suspended/expelled in any event.

Where the rules set out procedures for suspension or expulsion of undisciplined members, then providing those procedures are complied with, any decision to suspend or expel has the effect of stripping the member of all the rights and privileges of membership, either temporarily or permanently. The club officers are entitled to enforce the ban should the member try to enter the premises and exercise rights of membership. Further, the suspended member is incapable of exercising any powers of office (although not necessarily the right to nomination or election unless the rules specifically prevent a suspended member from being nominated or elected to a post during the period of suspension).

As a rule a suspended member remains liable to pay his or her subscription, because he or she is still a member, and it is reasonable that a suspension must not be open-ended. Periods of suspension should be laid out in the rules, but there must be a maximum. It is up to the members to decide in the rules, the maximum period of suspension, but a period greater than 12 months would seem excessive. If the conduct complained of warrants a greater period, then it probably warrants expulsion.

At the end of a period of suspension the suspended person is entitled to enjoy all the privileges of membership once more. It is for the members to decide whether a person who has been expelled from membership may, at some later time, re-apply for membership, and to incorporate their decision into the club rules. The rules may allow for a rehabilitation period, but they are more likely to provide that a person who has been expelled is not eligible for membership in the future; were readmission to be contemplated after the passage of time, suspension would seem a more sensible penalty in the first place.

There is nothing in law to prevent a club from taking action on the basis of conduct that occurs away from club premises or that is of a type unconnected with the club or its activities. Many clubs adopt a rule that gives the committee the right to take action if the conduct of a member, in the opinion of the committee, renders that person unfit for membership or generally brings the club into disrepute. Such conduct might include conviction for a criminal offence (particularly if it is of the nature of public disorder or dishonesty), persistent refusal to comply with club rules, or rude or offensive behaviour towards staff or other members.

14.4 Procedures

As a general rule, the courts will not interfere with disciplinary action taken by a club if the procedures are fair and accord with the rules. Lord Denning put the point nicely in *Lee v Showmen's Guild* [1952] 1 All ER 1175 at 118:

> ... in the case of Social Clubs the rules usually empower the Committee to expel a member who, in their opinion, has been guilty of conduct detrimental to the club and this is a matter of opinion and nothing else. The Courts have no wish to sit on appeal from their decisions in such a matter any more and from the decisions of a family conference. They have nothing to do with social rights or social duties. On any expulsion they will see that there is fair play. They will see that the man has notice of the charge and a reasonable opportunity of being heard. They will see that the committee observe the procedure laid down by the rules, but will not otherwise interfere ...

If the club does not follow its own rules it will have acted unfairly and will be challenged.

Clubs must be conscious of the principles of natural justice in their deliberations and should set out a system that is fair by incorporating the following guidelines:

- the right to a fair (unbiased) hearing;

- the right to notice of any charge and to prepare a response;

- the right to be heard;

- the right not to be punished without law, ie no punishment without a fair application of the rules.

Thus a system should require notice to be given to the alleged offender of the details of the allegations. The alleged offender should have the opportunity to address the body that adjudicates on the matter. The adjudicating body should be required to notify the accused person of the decision taken in respect of the allegation and the reasons for its findings. Consideration ought also to be given to whether the accused person should have a right of appeal.

The rules of a club should specify who is to deal with allegations of misconduct. In most cases responsibility is given to a group of members appointed for the purpose, or to the management committee. If an appeal system is to be established, it is advisable for the initial hearing to be conducted by a panel of members appointed to deal with disciplinary matters. This would allow for an appeal to the management committee where the member in question is aggrieved by the decision taken by the panel of members. If the initial hearing is before the management committee, any appeal might have to be dealt with by the members in a general meeting, which would not be easy to manage.

14.5 Delegation of authority

Not every act of misconduct or indiscipline on the part of a member or guest is serious enough to justify disciplinary proceedings. Many incidents consist of breaches of club rules that can simply be drawn to the attention of the offender. Difficulties can arise if the rules of the club do not make clear who has the power to enforce the rules and the duty of members to comply with directions given by that person.

Officers and committee members usually have authority to ensure the club is operated on proper lines and that members comply with the rules. The members elect the officers and the committee members, and the officers and committee members, as a general rule, have authority to deal with breaches of rules and minor incidents of misbehaviour. In some cases it is sensible for enforcement powers to be delegated to others who are in a better position to exercise control on a day-to-day basis. Enforcement powers might, for example, be delegated to the club steward or bar manager.

Where the authority to ensure that club rules are complied with by members and guests has been delegated under the rules, members and guests are under a duty to comply with any request made or instruction given by the person having delegated powers. Failure to do so would amount to an act of misconduct since it would be a breach of club rules. The rules are in place for the benefit of the members generally. On joining the club and accepting the benefits of membership, every member is aware of the rules. Members contract with one another that they accept the rules and continue to be bound by them.

14.6 Damages following disciplinary action

A question arising from time to time is whether a member who has a grievance about the way club disciplinary procedures have been applied may sue the club for damages. For example, where a member is expelled from membership and believes that the expulsion was not justified, can the member sue the club for the damage claimed to have been suffered as a result of the withdrawal of membership rights?

There are several problems in the concept of a member suing a club. The first is that it is likely that a member would be prohibited from taking action against the club. As a general rule, a members' club has no legal identity. It consists of a body of people who come together for common purposes, thereby forming an unincorporated association. The club's property and other assets are owned by the members in equal shares and so if a member were allowed to sue he would, in effect, be suing himself.

The situation may be different in the case of a club incorporated by shares or guarantee or by virtue of registration under the Industrial and Provident Societies Act 1965. Here there may be a body that has a separate identity and is capable of being sued. It might be said, for example, that the club owes a duty of care to each of its members and that, if a member suffers injury or loss as a consequence of the club's negligence, the member may seek to recover damages.

Even where a club has a separate legal identity, it would be very difficult for a member to obtain damages in respect of a suspension or expulsion. The main problem would be in quantifying the loss. The member might be able to recover any 'unused' subscription but otherwise valuing the privileges of membership that have been lost would be far from easy.

As mentioned above, the courts do not usually interfere with matters of club discipline as long as the club rules have been complied with. In agreeing to abide by club rules, a member agrees to accept the authority of the disciplinary panel and abide by any decision it might reach.

Obviously, if a member felt that the action to remove him had not been taken in good faith, or was procedurally unfair, or in some way in excess of the authority of the rules, he may take action to preserve his position. Notionally, as a member of the club, with a temporal right in property (being a beneficial interest from time to time in the assets of the club and the fruits of membership) the member will have a right of action against the committee and trustees. His action will not generally sound in damages but will afford a remedy in declaratory relief and an injunction to ensure his membership is not further interfered with. Effectively, his case before the court is a form of action for breach of contract where he asks for the court to say to the committee 'You got this wrong for the following reasons ...' – the so-called declaratory relief; and an injunction to restore him to membership.

14.7   Guests

Most clubs cater for guests. They may be people brought to the premises by members of the club, or they may be members of affiliated organisations visiting under reciprocal arrangements which allow the use of club facilities. As mentioned at the beginning of this chapter, guests are expected to behave in a proper manner and to comply with club rules. When a guest is on club premises at the invitation of a club member, that member also has a duty to ensure that the guest behaves in an appropriate manner.

From a practical point of view a club would find it virtually impossible to discipline a guest. The officers of the club and the staff are, however, entitled to ask the guest to leave the premises if the guest misbehaves or refuses to comply with club rules. Steps may also be taken to ensure that the offender is not allowed to enter the premises in the future. In extreme cases, the member may be liable to disciplinary action for failing to control the guest.

Most clubs have a rule that limits the number of guests a member may introduce to the club on any single occasion. This rule serves two purposes. First, it ensures that, usually, the persons in attendance are mostly members. This, in turn, means that the members remain in control of their club. Next, the rule serves to demonstrate that the club is properly constituted and run as a members' club, that is, as a club owned by the members and run by them for their collective benefit. Plainly, the treatment of guests is now further complicated by the requirements for non-discriminatory treatment under Equality Act 2010, Pt 7. Nevertheless, where the conduct of a guest is egregious, regardless of his or her protected characteristics, the committee is entitled to take reasoned and proportionate action against him or her.

15 Staff

15.1 Introduction

While in some members' clubs the work to keep the operation running is done by members, in most clubs it is undertaken by employees. Many members' clubs are employers and so need to be aware of the law relating to employment. The officers and committee members are responsible for ensuring that the club complies with the law. Statutory provisions affect all stages of employment, from recruitment and appointment of staff, to conditions of employment, and on to termination of contracts. Discipline and the maintenance of order have to be dealt with in any club and those who are responsible for those matters need to be aware of the statutory constraints.

The rules of a club may contain specific provisions relating to the employment of staff, but if not, the committee members become impliedly responsible for employment matters. It follows also that under the law of agency the individual committee members may become liable for the pay of employees, as they would under any other contract. It is therefore important that decisions on recruitment and employment are dealt with in the rules and that no appointment is made without the concurrence of the relevant committee or, if need be, the membership.

The law relating to employment is wide and complex and it is beyond the scope of this book to deal with it comprehensively, but in this chapter, some of the more important points are highlighted. Since the last edition of this book, employment law has changed considerably. The Equality Act 2010 passed onto the statute book on 8 April 2010. Whilst this is a formidable body of law, it ultimately has the effect of consolidating the nine separate Acts and bodies of regulations which governed discrimination law in the United Kingdom (although there is scope for slightly differing provision in Scotland). Most of the measures in the Act came into force in October 2010.

15.2   Equality Act 2010

Under previous law, it was illegal to discriminate against any person in the selection and recruitment of staff on any of the following grounds:

- sex and equal pay: Sex Discrimination Act 1975; Equal Pay Act 1970;

- sexual orientation: Employment Equality (Sexual Orientation) Regulations 2003 (SI 2003/1661); Equality Act 2006;

- gender reassignment: Sex Discrimination Act 1975;

- race: Race Relations Act 1976;

- religion or belief: Employment Equality (Religion or Belief) Regulations 2003 (SI 2003/1660);

- disability: Disability Discrimination Act 1995;

- age: Employment Equality (Age) Regulations 2006 (SI 2006/1031).

The Equality Act 2010 repealed all of this law and for the first time consolidated the various provision under one Act. For an employer there are various changes which need to be considered, all of which centre on the definition of a series of protected characteristics, of relevance to the whole population.

Section 4 provides that the following protected characteristics apply:

- age;

- disability;

- gender reassignment;

- marriage and civil partnership;

- pregnancy and maternity;

- race;

- religion or belief;

- sex;

- sexual orientation.

For the first time a series of discriminatory practices are defined in the Act. These definitions are drawn from experience arising under the outgoing regulations and case law.

15.3   Direct discrimination

Under Equality Act 2010, s 13 direct discrimination is described as:

> (1) A person (A) discriminates against another (B) if, because of a protected characteristic, A treats B less favourably than A treats or would treat others.

Insofar as it is relevant to the workplace the guidance to this section also provides that:

- for age, different treatment that is justified as a proportionate means of meeting a legitimate aim is not direct discrimination;

- in relation to disability it is not discrimination to treat a disabled person more favourably than a person who is not disabled;

- racial segregation is always discriminatory.

Thus, if a club were to advertise for a barman, a female applicant might have a claim for sex discrimination if she could show that she was treated differently from other applicants for the job and that her treatment was due to the fact that she is a woman. Her claim would be unlikely to succeed, however, if the employer could show that, despite the wording of the advertisement, all applicants were treated in the same way and that the fact that she was not appointed was for reasons unrelated to her sex, for example, the greater experience of the person appointed.

Employers need also to be aware of the issues of associative and perceptive discrimination. Because the person complaining of the discrimination does not need to have the actual characteristic under s 13(1) they may still have been discriminated against because they are associated with one of the characteristics (ie the mother of a disabled child is seen as less reliable, or is subject to prejudicial or hurtful comment; or an employee who is a carer for elderly parents is not granted the same flexibility as parents of children). In cases of perceptive discrimination a person might be quite falsely perceived to have one of the protected characteristics and on the basis of that misapprehension is directly discriminated against.

Under s 14, discrimination under a combination of protected characteristics arises where:

> (1) A person (A) discriminates against another (B) if, because of a combination of two relevant protected characteristics, A treats B less favourably than A treats or would treat a person who does not share either of those characteristics.
>
> (2) The relevant protected characteristics are—

(a) age;

(b) disability;

(c) gender reassignment;

(d) race

(e) religion or belief;

(f) sex;

(g) sexual orientation.

The nuisance addressed by this section is best illustrated by the example given in the statutory guidance, thus:

> A black woman has been passed over for promotion to work on reception because her employer thinks black women do not perform well in customer service roles. Because the employer can point to a white woman of equivalent qualifications and experience who has been appointed to the role in question, as well as a black man of equivalent qualifications and experience in a similar role, the woman may need to be able to compare her treatment because of race and sex combined to demonstrate that she has been subjected to less favourable treatment because of her employer's prejudice against black women.

Section 15 deals with discrimination arising from disability:

(1) A person (A) discriminates against a disabled person (B) if—

(a) A treats B unfavourably because of something arising in consequence of B's disability, and

(b) A cannot show that .the treatment is a proportionate means of achieving a legitimate aim.

(2) Subsection (1) does not apply if A shows that A did not know, and could not reasonably have been expected to know, that B had the disability.

This section is intended to prevent discrimination arising from or in consequence of, a person's disability, such as the need to take a period of disability-related absence. It is, however, possible to justify such treatment if it can be shown to be a proportionate means of achieving a legitimate aim. For this type of discrimination to occur, the employer or other person must know, or reasonably be expected to know, that the disabled person has a disability.

Section 16 deals with gender reassignment discrimination in cases of absence from work:

(1) This section has effect for the purposes of the application of Part 5 (work) to the protected characteristic of gender reassignment.

(2) A person (A) discriminates against a transsexual person (B) if, in relation to an absence of B's that is because of gender reassignment, A treats B less favourably than A would treat B if—

    (a) B's absence was because of sickness or injury, or

    (b) B's absence was for some other reason and it is not reasonable for B to be treated less favourably.

(3) A person's absence is because of gender reassignment if it is because the person is proposing to undergo, is undergoing or has undergone the process (or part of the process) mentioned in section 7(1).

This section defines discrimination against transsexual people as occurring where they are treated less favourably for being absent from work because they propose to undergo, are undergoing or have undergone gender reassignment than they would be treated if they were absent because they were ill or injured.

Section 18 defines pregnancy and maternity discrimination in the work place:

(1) This section has effect for the purposes of the application of Part 5 (work) to the protected characteristic of pregnancy and maternity.

(2) A person (A) discriminates against a woman if, in the protected period in relation to a pregnancy of hers, A treats her unfavourably—

    (a) because of the pregnancy, or

    (b) because of illness suffered by her as a result of it.

(3) A person (A) discriminates against a woman if A treats her unfavourably because she is on compulsory maternity leave.

(4) A person (A) discriminates against a woman if A treats her unfavourably because she is exercising or seeking to exercise, or has exercised or sought to exercise, the right to ordinary or additional maternity leave.

(5) For the purposes of subsection (2), if the treatment of a woman is in implementation of a decision taken in the protected period, the treatment is to be regarded as occurring in that period (even if the implementation is not until after the end of that period).

(6) The protected period, in relation to a woman's pregnancy, begins when the pregnancy begins, and ends—

    (a) if she has the right to ordinary and additional maternity leave, at the end of the additional maternity leave period or (if earlier) when she returns to work after the pregnancy;

    (b) if she does not have that right, at the end of the period of 2 weeks beginning with the end of the pregnancy.

(7) Section 13, so far as relating to sex discrimination, does not apply to treatment of a woman in so far as—

(a) it is in the protected period in relation to her and is for a reason mentioned in paragraph (a) or (b) of subsection (2), or

(b) it is for a reason mentioned in subsection (3) or (4).

This section defines what it means to discriminate in the workplace because of a woman's pregnancy or pregnancy-related illness (s 18(2)(a)(b)), or because she takes or wants maternity leave (s 18(4). The protection from these types of discrimination is provided during the pregnancy and any statutory maternity leave to which she is entitled. During this period, these types of discrimination cannot be treated as sex discrimination (s 18(7)).

15.4 Indirect discrimination

Section 19 defines indirect discrimination as:

(1) A person (A) discriminates against another (B) if A applies to B a provision, criterion or practice which is discriminatory in relation to a relevant protected characteristic of B's.

(2) For the purposes of subsection (1), a provision, criterion or practice is discriminatory in relation to a relevant protected characteristic of B's if—

(a) A applies, or would apply, it to persons with whom B does not share the characteristic,

(b) it puts, or would put, persons with whom B shares the characteristic at a particular disadvantage when compared with persons with whom B does not share it,

(c) it puts, or would put, B at that disadvantage, and

(d) A cannot show it to be a proportionate means of achieving a legitimate aim.

(3) The relevant protected characteristics are—

age;

disability;

gender reassignment;

marriage and civil partnership;

race;

religion or belief;

sex;

sexual orientation.

Indirect discrimination occurs when a policy or rule applicable to all employees has an effect which particularly disadvantages staff or applicants with a protected characteristic. When a particular group is disadvantaged in this way, a person in that group is indirectly discriminated against if he or she is put at that disadvantage, unless the person applying the policy can justify it. Thus a requirement for mandatory Saturday work may unnecessarily discriminate against a Jewish employee or applicant. Indirect discrimination applies to all the protected characteristics, apart from pregnancy and maternity.

Examples of factors which have been held to be requirements or conditions include refusal to employ a person with young children since this would affect considerably more married than unmarried persons (*Thorndyke v Bell Fruit (North Central) Ltd* [1979] IRLR 1); and refusal to hire persons resident in a particular postal district where 50% of the population were black (*Hussein v Saints Complete House Furnishers Ltd* [1979] IRLR 337).

15.4.1 The requirement to make reasonable adjustments for disabled staff/applicants

Equality Act 2010, s 20 covers employer's duties to make reasonable adjustments to accommodate disabled staff and applicants. The section anticipates three distinct requirements to prevent disabled staff or applicants being at a significant disadvantage:

- the first requirement (s 20(3)) covers changing the way things are done (such as changing a practice);

- the second (s 20(4)) covers making changes to the built environment, such as providing access to a building, include removing, altering or providing a reasonable means of avoiding the physical feature, where it would be reasonable to do so. Physical features are further defined in s 20(10) as:

    (a)   a feature arising from the design or construction of a building,

    (b)   a feature of an approach to, exit from or access to a building,

    (c)   a fixture or fitting, or furniture, furnishings, materials, equipment or other chattels, in or on premises, or

    (d)   any other physical element or quality.

- the third requirement (s 20(5)) covers providing auxiliary aids and services (such as providing special computer software or providing a different service).

The section (s 20(6)) makes clear that where the first or third requirements involves the way in which information is provided, a reasonable step includes providing that information in an accessible format.

Section 20(7) also makes clear that, except where the Act states otherwise, it would never be reasonable for a person bound by the duty to pass on the costs of complying with it to an individual disabled person.

Section 60 prevents a recruiting employer from making enquiry of an applicant's medical history before offering them employment.

The only permitted health-related questions at the recruitment stage are those required to:

- discover whether a job applicant would be able to participate in an assessment to test their suitability for the work;

- make reasonable adjustments to enable the disabled person to participate in the recruitment process;

- discover whether a job applicant would be able to undertake a function that is intrinsic to the job, with reasonable adjustments in place as required;

- monitor diversity in applications for jobs;

- support positive action in employment for disabled people; and

- enable an employer to identify suitable candidates for a job where there is a genuine occupational requirement for the person to be disabled.

A breach of s 60 is actionable by the Equality and Human Rights Commission.

15.5   Harassment and victimisation

Under s 26(1) the Act defines harassment as:

> Unwanted conduct related to a relevant protected characteristic, which has the purpose or effect of violating an individual's dignity or creating an intimidating, hostile, degrading, humiliating or offensive environment for that individual.

Section 26(2) extends the definition to harassment of a sexual nature or in relation to gender re-assignment. In compliance with the Act and the EU Equal Treatment Directive, harassment is extended to all protected characteristics except marital status and will render employers potentially liable for the conduct of third parties – such as abusive customers. The latter provisions are set out in s 40.

15.5.1 Victimisation

Under s 27 an employer (A) is liable for victimisation when an employee is treated badly because they have made or are anticipated to make a protected act. For the purposes of this section a protected act is defined as:

(1)   bringing proceedings under this Act;

(2)   giving evidence or information in connection with proceedings under this Act;

(3)   doing any other thing for the purposes of or in connection with this Act;

(4)   making an allegation (whether or not express) that A or another person has contravened this Act.

Victimisation has not occurred if the employee has maliciously made or supported an untrue complaint.

15.6   Recruitment and employment

Equality Act 2010, Pt 5 deals specifically with recruitment and employment. Section 39 makes it unlawful for an employer to engage in any of the above discriminatory conduct in relation to employment and recruitment. The section also imposes the reasonable adjustments duty set out in s 20 on employers in respect of disabled employees and applicants. Section 41 extends similar provisions to the treatment of contract workers.

Employers will also need to be aware of the host of other sections relating to equal pay and equality of terms to be found in Pt 3 of the Act. Further discussion of these terms is beyond the remit of this edition.

Enforcement of the Pt 5 provisions lies with the Employment Tribunal, whose powers are set out in s 120 in Pt 9 of the Act. The Tribunal has powers under the Act at s 124 to:

(1)   make a declaration as to the rights of the complainant and the respondent in relation to the matters to which the proceedings relate;

(2)   order the respondent to pay compensation to the complainant;

(3)   make an appropriate recommendation.

An appropriate recommendation is a recommendation to an employer to obviate any further harm to the work force and should be ordered to occur within a certain time frame, in default of which, a compensation order may be made or, if one already exists, increased.

Compensation is measured on the same tortious scale as is available to county courts under s 119.

This is a complex and dynamic area of law and it is anticipated that there will be no less activity in the courts and tribunals under the new Act. Club committees are advised to follow the statutory guidance in the Act itself. This can be found online at www.opsi.gov.uk/acts/acts2010/ukpga_20100015_en_1.

In addition there is now an ACAS guide, *The Equality Act – What's new for employers*, which is available on the ACAS website at www.acas.org.uk/CHttpHandler.ashx?id=2833&p=0.

Further information is available from the Equality and Human Rights Commission on its website at www.equalityhumanrights.com/.

15.7   Contracts of employment and job descriptions

The contract of employment, whilst now heavily regulated by statute and secondary legislation is still founded in the common law of contract. The contract sets out the relationship between the employer and the employee. A contract of employment, like any other contract, comes into being when the terms of an offer of employment made by one party, the employer, are accepted by the other party, the employee. The popular concept that to be binding a contract must be in writing is a myth. The terms of a contract of employment are often oral, or deduced from the conduct of the parties or from secondary sources such as letters and job descriptions. In addition, certain terms may be implied, while some may be imposed by statute. Statutory terms are implied or imposed by an Act of Parliament or statutory instrument, and will include for instance equality of pay, minimum wage and minimum notice periods. It is generally unlawful for the employer to attempt to contract out of these provisions.

Employers are under a duty under Employment Rights Act 1996, s 1 to provide employees with a written statement of certain terms of their employment. Such statements must be provided within 2 months of the commencement of employment and should include the following terms:

(1) the names of the employer and employee;

(2) the date when the employment began;

(3) the date on which the employee's period of continuous employment began (taking into account any employment with a previous employer which counts towards that period);

(4) the scale or rate of remuneration or the method of calculating remuneration;

(5) the intervals at which remuneration is paid (that is, weekly, monthly or other specified intervals);

(6) any terms and conditions relating to hours of work (including any terms and conditions relating to normal working hours);

(7) any terms and conditions relating to any of the following:

(a) entitlement to holidays, including public holidays, and holiday pay (the particulars given being sufficient to enable the employee's entitlement, including any entitlement to accrued holiday pay on the termination of employment, to be precisely calculated),

(b) incapacity for work due to sickness or injury, including any provision for sick pay, and pensions, and

(c) pension schemes,

(8) the length of notice which the employee is obliged to give and entitled to receive to terminate his contract of employment;

(9) the title of the job which the employee is employed to do or a brief description of the work for which he is employed;

(10) where the employment is not intended to be permanent, the period for which it is expected to continue or, if it is for a fixed term, the date when it is to end;

(11) either the place of work or, where the employee is required or permitted to work at various places, an indication of that and of the address of the employer;

(12) any collective agreements which directly affect the terms and conditions of the employment including, where the employer is not a party, the persons by whom they were made;

(13) other terms relating to work overseas.

A wise employer not only supplies this statement of limited terms but also enters into a contract that contains, in addition to the obligatory terms, all the other terms and conditions of the agreement that will govern the future working relationship between the parties.

15.8 Variation of terms

It may be that circumstances change and that the club would like to alter the terms of employment or job description of a member of staff. Once made, though, it may not be easy to change the terms of a contract. The general rule is that the terms of a contract, including the job description where appropriate, can be changed only with the agreement of both parties. Careful thought should be given to the wording of a job description in the first place, especially if some flexibility may be needed as the club develops. Provided it is not unreasonable, a 'catch-all' condition of employment may prove invaluable. A concluding sentence in the job description to the effect that, in addition to the specified tasks, the employee will be expected to carry out any other tasks that the employer may reasonably ask the employee to undertake is not uncommon. Of course, the request will not be reasonable if the work to be undertaken is specialist work beyond the competence of the employee in question. Enforced variation of terms by dismissal and re-engagement under a new contract may give rise to a claim for breach of contract and is to be avoided.

Further guidance is available from ACAS in the publication, *Varying a Contract of Employment*, which is available on the ACAS website at www.acas.org.uk/CHttpHandler.ashx?id=316.

15.9 Termination of employment

15.9.1 By notice

Unless a contract is for a fixed term, in which case it comes to an end on the expiry of the specified period, employment is taken to be for an indefinite period but subject to termination by the giving of reasonable notice. Often the period of notice to be given, by either the employer or the employee, is one of the matters agreed between the parties at the beginning of the employment. Where there is such an agreement, the period should be set out in the written particulars of employment.

In the absence of an agreed period of notice, the law is that a 'reasonable' period of notice must be given. What is reasonable in any particular case depends on the employment in question. In many instances, the payment interval is taken to be a reasonable period. For example, weekly wage earners are usually required to give and entitled to receive one week's notice, while in the case of a person employed on a monthly salary, one month's notice is usually deemed reasonable. The importance of the particular job to the employer's organisation may demand a longer period in which to find a replacement, but in such a case it is to be expected that the period would be agreed in advance and set out in the terms of employment.

The Employment Rights Act 1996 provides for a minimum period of notice. An employer must give an employee a minimum of one week's notice if the employee has been employed for between one month and 2 years; and an additional week's notice for each year of employment thereafter, up to a maximum of 12 weeks where employment has lasted for 12 years or more. An employee who has been in employment for more than one month must give a minimum of one week's notice.

The statute does not prevent the parties from agreeing to waive the statutory period of notice, or from agreeing a payment in lieu of notice. Nor does the statute affect the right of an employer to terminate a contract without the statutory notice where the employee has been guilty of misconduct.

Whether an employer is entitled to make a payment in lieu of notice if the employee wishes to work out his notice is uncertain (*Marshall (Cambridge) Ltd v Hamblin* EAT/705/91). It is clear that where the right to notice is waived, the right to payment in lieu of notice is lost (*Trotter v Forth Ports Authority* [1991] IRLR 419 and *Baldwin v British Coal Corporation* [1995] IRLR 139).

During periods of notice the rate of payment made to the employee must be the usual weekly or monthly rate. This is so even if the employee does not work during the period.

15.9.2 Following a breach of contract

A contract of employment may come to an end if there is a fundamental breach of the contract terms. Such breaches may consist of a breach of a term or condition which destroys the implied trust between the parties and/or:

- is considered by the parties to be vital;

- has such serious consequences that the other party to the contract is deprived of that which he contracted for;

- demonstrates that the other party does not intend to continue to be bound by one or more of the terms or conditions.

Generally, where an employer is aware of a fundamental breach of the terms of the contract and decides in any event to carry on employing, he loses the right subsequently to dismiss the employee for that breach of contract.

15.9.3 By dismissal

The law recognises that, as a general rule, a dismissal is lawful providing the proper notice is given. There are exceptional circumstances which may affect this, but they are unlikely to arise in relation to members' clubs.

In certain circumstances an employee's contract may be terminated without notice, that is, he may be summarily dismissed. For summary dismissal to be justified, it is necessary to show that the conduct complained of is such that the employee has been shown to disregard the essential conditions of his contract of employment (*Laws v London Chronicle (Indicator Newspapers) Ltd* [1959] 1 WLR 698). Examples of gross misconduct are theft from the employer or other act of dishonesty against the employer, and gross insubordination.

There may be a case of 'constructive dismissal' if an employee resigns because conduct on the part of the employer gives rise, in the opinion of the employee, to a fundamental breakdown in the trust that should exist between employer and staff. Where constructive dismissal is found to have occurred, the employee is entitled to compensation and/or damages, even though he was the person who brought the contract of employment to an end.

Employers should take advice on disciplinary matters generally and are required to observe the ACAS Code of Practice 1 – Disciplinary and Grievance Procedure, which is a statutory guidance. If an employee or employer 'unreasonably' fails to abide by the principles of the code, this can result in an employee's compensation being increased or reduced by a tribunal by up to 25%.

The Code is available to download from the ACAS website at www.acas.org.uk/CHttpHandler.ashx?id=1047.

15.10 Working time

The UK government has adopted European directives controlling working time and the employment of young workers. The terms of these directives have been incorporated in the Working Time Regulations 1998 (SI 1998/1833). These regulations apply to workers and employees. There are certain exceptions and exemptions in the regulations, but none that would be relevant to members' clubs.

The general purpose of the regulations is that any person who works for another, whether or not on the basis of a contract of employment, should have the protection of the European directives. The position of persons who work on a casual or agency basis is not entirely clear, usually because it is uncertain whether there is an employer against whom any proceedings may properly be taken. Any application to a tribunal or county court to enforce the regulations would be determined on the basis of the facts of the particular case.

15.10.1 Limit on hours

The object of the Working Time Regulations 1998 is to safeguard the health and safety of workers. The principal safeguard is a limit on the number of hours that an employee may be asked to work in any week. In the case of an adult worker, the maximum number of hours that may be worked in any week is 48. However, the limit applies to the average number of hours worked over a 17-week reference period. A worker may lawfully be asked to work for more than 48 hours in a particular week as long as the average over the reference period does not exceed 48 hours. By way of example, if a worker puts in 40 hours a week for 12 weeks, then works 10 hours' overtime for the next 5 weeks, the average working time over the reference period would be within the limit laid down by the regulations:

$$(40 \times 12) + (50 \times 5) = 730$$

$$730 \div 17 = 42.94 \text{ hours per week}$$

For the purpose of calculating the average number of hours worked, certain days are 'excluded days'. Annual holiday, sick leave, maternity leave and any time during which the employee does not work are excluded days. There is a formula for making the appropriate calculation: $A + B - C$, where:

- A is the number of hours worked during the reference period;

- B is the number of hours worked in the days added to the end of the reference period to account for days that are excluded; and

- C is the number of weeks making up the reference period.

For example, if a worker works 700 hours during the reference period of 17 weeks and then works 70 hours during days added due to excluded days, the hours worked are within the prescribed limits:

$$700 \ (A) + 70 \ (B) = 770$$

$$770 \div 17 \ (C) = 45.29 \text{ hours per week}$$

The Regulations allow individual workers to opt out. The 48 hours rule can be disapplied in individual cases, but only if the employee consents and the agreement is in writing. Certain classes of worker are also exempt, but these exemptions have no relevance to clubs.

15.10.2 Holidays and rest periods

The Working Time Regulations 1998 make provision not only for maximum working hours, but also for regular breaks during working periods and for holidays. The breaks to which an employee is entitled are, in broad terms, as follows. Where an adult worker's daily working time is more than 6 hours, the worker is entitled to a rest break. In the absence of any collective or workforce agreement, the rest period is 20 minutes. The worker is entitled to spend that period of time away from the usual workstation. Where a worker is employed for periods in excess of 6 hours, it may be appropriate for the break entitlement to be increased in the light of ongoing health and safety obligations. If a worker is working for, say, 9 hours a day, it might be appropriate to have a break of 30 minutes, or two breaks of 15 minutes each.

All workers who are within the scope of the Working Time Regulations 1998 are entitled to paid annual leave. Under the Working Time Regulations 1998 (as amended), workers (including part-timers and most agency and freelance workers) have the right to:

* 5.6 weeks' paid leave each year (from 1 April 2009);

* payment for untaken statutory leave entitlement on termination of employment.

Many workers who already get contractual leave which is more than 5.6 weeks (28 days). Their entitlement is unchanged, and is certainly not amenable to downward adjustment by employers.

15.10.3 The leave year

Employers and employees may agree between themselves when the leave year is to begin. It may be included in the contract of employment and may be determined by the exigencies of the business. In the absence of any such agreement, the leave year is taken to begin on 1 October in the case of a worker whose employment began before 1 October 1998. Otherwise, the leave year begins on the date the employment commenced.

15.11 The national minimum wage

A minimum wage came into effect on 1 April 1999 when the National Minimum Wage Regulations 1999 (SI 1999/584) came into force. Under the Regulations, persons who have attained the qualifying ages are entitled to receive a minimum hourly wage. The Regulations give effect to European directives on minimum wages.

With effect from October 2010, the standard national minimum wage is £5.93 an hour for workers aged 21 and over. Certain persons, including workers aged between 18 and 21, qualify for a minimum wage of £4.92 per hour. Workers aged below 18 who are no longer of compulsory school age qualify for a minimum wage of £3.64 per hour.

HM Revenue and Customs (HMRC) keeps an eye on minimum wage provisions since it is in a good position to monitor payments and to spot breaches of the Regulations. HMRC may well draw the attention of an offending employer to the regulatory obligations. A worker who is not being paid the correct minimum hourly rate can apply to an industrial tribunal to enforce the correct rate.

An employee who gives up employment because the employer does not pay the minimum wage would have a strong case for constructive dismissal before a tribunal. In addition, since the duty to comply with the Regulations may be deemed to be an implied term of a contract of employment, an aggrieved employee may be able to claim in the county court for damages for breach of contract.

15.12 Health and safety

See also Chapter 17, for a club's duty as an employer in respect of health and safety at work, and to conduct risk assessments.

PART SIX

LIABILITIES

16 Liabilities

16.1 Introduction

Anyone responsible for the management of a club needs to be aware of the sources of liability attaching to it. In considering these responsibilities it is as well to consider all of the classes of people who are likely to be on club premises from time to time – thus members and their guests, children, tradesmen, utilities, bins, deliveries, post, etc. The list is endless.

Whereas it has been seen above that the duties owed to members by a club arise in contract (*Robertson v Ridley* [1989] 1 WLR 872, CA), the common law and statute fix the owners and operators of club premises with obligations towards every person who is likely to enter the premises or use the club's facilities – whether or not they have been invited. Anyone who suffers an injury as a result of dangerous premises, or encountering a hazard on the premises may seek damages. Further, the club has specific responsibilities if it serves food and drink under the relevant legislation, and the club is further regulated in its responsibilities towards its workforce.

The club must carry a level of insurance sufficient to cover any foreseeable liability, and should take advice from its broker over the extent of cover required. By law there is a requirement for a minimum £5 million employer's liability (see below).

16.2 Occupiers' liability – duty of care to members and guests

The owner and occupier of any premises is under a duty to ensure that anyone visiting the premises is safe. The common law had distinguished between invitees, in whose visit the occupier had some interest (eg guest), and licensees, who came simply by express or implied permission (eg postman). The Occupiers' Liability Act 1957 did away with that distinction and now the law considers merely occupiers and visitors.

16.2.1 Occupiers

The occupier is any person who has a sufficient degree of control over premises, thus in *Wheat v Lacon* [1966] 1 All ER 582 both the landlord and tenant of a pub owed a duty of care to a guest injured on the stairs.

In the case of an unincorporated club, it will be the case that a trustee/officer will be the occupier and he will perforce be the defendant in any subsequent action.

16.2.2 Visitors

Under Occupiers' Liability Act 1957, s 1(2), the occupier owes a common duty of care to all lawful visitors (*Stone v Taffe* [1974] 3 All ER 1016). For the purposes of the 1957 Act, members and guests of a club would both be treated as visitors, as they are effectively the invitees of the club.

16.2.3 Common duty of care

Under Occupiers' Liability Act 1957, s 2(2), there is a common duty of care to take such care as is reasonable in all the circumstances to see that the visitor will be reasonably safe in using the premises for the purposes for which he or she is invited or permitted to be there.

However, under s 2(3) that duty is qualified in two important respects:

- Children are less likely to have regard to their own safety than adults (s 2(3)(a)). Therefore, if a club admits children to the premises the child visitor must be reasonably safe (*Jolley v Sutton LBC* [2000] 3 All ER 409). Children often fail to see the danger inherent in attractions such as pools, rides and mechanical devices. It is critical that clubs should take special care to minimise the risk of harm arising to children from these features. Whilst such advice may seem trite, it bears repeating that children do not or cannot read safety warnings. It follows that in order to discharge its duty of care towards children in particular both children and their parents should be made expressly aware of any hazard. Where hazards are identified they should be made as safe as possible.

- An occupier may expect that a person, in the exercise of his trade, appreciates and guards against any risks ordinarily incident to that trade so far as the occupier leaves him free to do so (s 2(3)(b)). Thus an electrician, called to the premises to repair plant in the cellar, or a roofer called to fix a skylight, will be expected at law to appreciate the hazards inherent to the task he has been asked to do

16.2.4 Warnings

Where harm is caused to a visitor by a danger of which he had been warned by the occupier, the warning does not automatically absolve the occupier from liability, unless in all the circumstances, it was enough to enable the visitor to be reasonably safe (s 2(4)(a)). However, this does not mean that a member or the parent of a young member or guest can simply pay lip service to any warning given by the club and expect those responsible for the premises to pick up the pieces and pay out. So long as the club has made clear a hazard in clear language, visitors (whether the parents of children or otherwise) must take note of the warning and conduct themselves or control their children accordingly.

Ultimately, if a visitor or guest is to succeed in a claim against the club he or she will need to show that the club has failed in its duty of care. To succeed in a claim for damages or compensation for injuries suffered on club premises, the claimant would have to satisfy the court that the club had, in some way, failed in its duty of care. If the club is able to show that it took all reasonable precautions to guard against the risk of injury and to prevent members and guests from coming to harm, it will be in a strong position to contest any claim. Whether the precautions taken were reasonable, in all the circumstances, would be a matter for a court to decide on the facts.

Certain steps, however, go a long way to countering any claim for negligence. First, clubs should take the precaution of carrying out regular risk assessments. The club premises should be examined to identify any hazardous features of the property which should be guarded against, if not removed. The findings of these risk assessments should be recorded, as should the steps taken to remove or minimise each risk. Production of such a record would be of great assistance in any proceedings that might be brought. Risk assessment is considered in greater depth later in this chapter.

Another precaution a club might reasonably take would be to post warning notices that cannot easily be eradicated in conspicuous places adjacent to any hazard. Clearly exhibiting a notice that draws attention to a hazard or disclaims liability for injuries caused by it would not, in itself, exonerate the club from liability for injury or damage caused by it, but it may considerably reduce the club's liability if a claim for compensation were made. If it can be shown that the club has been negligent in any way or otherwise failed in its duty of care, it may still be held liable and ordered to pay damages or compensation to the claimant.

Generally, it is advisable to post warning and disclaimer notices where appropriate, because their presence will make it more difficult, if a claim is made, to show that the club was negligent. Even if a degree of negligence is proved, such warnings may well mitigate the extent of the club's liability.

16.3 Occupiers' liability – duty of care to others

A club's duty to safeguard members and guests has been discussed above. A club also has a general duty as the occupier of premises to prevent harm to others who may come onto the premises. The duty of care extends to predictable harm that may be caused to persons outside club premises as a result of the activities that take place on the premises.

Many people, other than members or guests, have occasion to come onto a club's premises. Workers, trades people, representatives of retailers or wholesalers, visiting entertainers and members of visiting sports teams may all visit the premises from time to time. All these people are visitors for the purposes of the Occupiers' Liability Act 1957 and the club, as occupier of the premises, has a duty of care in respect of them. Accordingly, it must take all reasonable steps to ensure such persons do not come to harm as a result of the condition of the premises or any activity carried out on the premises. In certain circumstances, the duty of care may extend to persons who find themselves in the vicinity of the club's premises.

It may be difficult to accept the proposition that a club, as occupier of its premises, has a duty of care to persons who venture onto them unlawfully, but the law does extend the duty of care to such persons. It may not be as onerous in the case of trespassers, but obvious dangers should be guarded against. A good example of the fact that it is necessary to safeguard trespassers from predictable harm may be found in the warnings frequently posted on premises guarded by dogs at night.

An occupier's duty in respect of persons other than visitors is set out in the Occupiers' Liability Act 1984. This Act provides that an occupier owes a duty of care to persons other than visitors in respect of certain specified risks. These are the risks of suffering injury on the premises by reason of any danger due to the state of the premises, or to things done or omitted to be done on them. Liability arises if:

- the occupier is aware of the danger or has reasonable grounds to believe that it exists;

- the occupier knows or has reasonable grounds to believe that the other is in the vicinity of the danger concerned, or that that other may come into the vicinity of the danger, whether or not that person has lawful authority to be in that vicinity; and

- the risk is one against which, in all the circumstances of the case, the occupier may reasonably be expected to offer the other person some protection.

It is these provisions that bring trespassers and persons who may be passing the club premises within the scope of the occupier's duty of care. The extent of the occupier's liability is to take such care as is reasonable in all the circumstances to see that the person does not suffer injury by reason of the danger concerned.

The liability which a club may have in respect of damage, injury or loss suffered by persons outside the premises has already been mentioned. The common law duty of care applies and, consequently, it is incumbent on all clubs to examine their activities and to take steps to protect passers-by from any risks from those activities. If it can be shown that the damage or injury suffered was caused by the club's negligence, the club will be liable.

Where, for example, the access road to club premises passes over a public footpath, the surface of the access road should be maintained in a good state of repair. Otherwise, an injury caused if a passer-by stumbles or falls on a damaged or uneven surface may give rise to an order for the payment of compensation. Other examples of potential danger include damage or injury caused by a golf or cricket ball, struck on club premises, striking a passer-by or a passing vehicle.

The Occupiers' Liability Act 1984 may come into play in other circumstances. An obvious example is where masonry, or other fixtures forming part of club premises, causes damage or injury by falling into the street because of inadequate maintenance.

16.4   Noise – causing a public noise nuisance

Clubs which include among their qualifying activities the provision of musical and other entertainment should ensure that the noise emanating from their premises is controlled at an acceptable level. The effect of noise from club activities on people who live and work in the vicinity of the premises may lead to intervention by environmental health officers.

Noise is one of the pollutants referred to in the Control of Pollution Act 1974. Local authority environmental health officers have power under the Act to take action under Environmental Protection Act 1990, ss 79 and 80 if they believe that noise emanating from any premises has reached such a level as to constitute a statutory noise nuisance. Most authorities operate a 24-hour emergency service that provides for an officer of the authority to respond to complaints about excessive noise at any time of the day or night.

A local authority may serve a notice (an abatement notice) on any person whom it considers to be responsible for a noise nuisance, if it appears that the noise level emanating from premises is not acceptable and that a reduction of the level is practicable at reasonable cost and would afford a public benefit.

A local authority is empowered under the Control of Pollution Act 1974 to designate an area as a noise abatement zone. If it does so, it must keep a register of all measurements of noise levels emanating from premises in that area. The level of noise recorded in the register in respect of any premises may not be exceeded unless the local authority has given its written consent. If the noise coming from premises exceeds this level, the person responsible (in the case of a members' club, the chairman or secretary) is guilty of an offence. The penalty is a fine not exceeding £5,000, together with a daily fine of £50 for each day on which the offence continues after the date of the conviction.

Further, Clean Neighbourhoods and Environment Act 2005, s 84 and Sch 1 extend the Noise Act 1996 to licensed premises and premises with a temporary event notice. Whilst many clubs will not be licensed premises, a great many will routinely apply for temporary event notices, and in that case the new regime will bite.

The statutes allow local authorities to take proceedings against licensed premises which exceed the permitted level for noise, with a maximum fine of up to £5,000 upon summary conviction or payment of a fixed penalty notice of £500 within 14 days. There is further provision for the confiscation of noise-making apparatus

Similar powers are contained in Anti-Social Behaviour Act 2003, s 40, which gives either the local authority's chief executive or an authorised environmental health officer, the power to close premises which cause a public noise nuisance. The notice will apply for a specified period not exceeding 24 hours (starting at the time the club officer receives notice) and is clearly aimed at taking the heat out of situations which represent a public order problem. Again, this power applies to licensed premises or premises operating under a temporary event notice. It is a criminal offence to allow the premises to open when a closure order is in place. If the premises are re-opened during the currency of the notice the offence is punishable on summary conviction by a maximum fine of £20,000 and or a maximum prison sentence of 3 months.

If club premises are the regular subject of complaints by the public it is inevitable that the licensing authority will take an interest and may seek to review the club premises certificate, because of the nuisance being occasioned to the public. Clubs need to be aware of the possible sources of annoyance occasioned by entertainments and amplified music and should seek to mitigate any potential disturbance by actively managing the ways in which noise is produced. Many local authorities advocate the preparation and implementation of a noise management plan, although this is not compulsory. Such audits are useful as they allow clubs to consider all those sources of incidental noise which, whilst part of the club routine, may be a source of annoyance to neighbours. For instance, people drinking and talking over a game of bowls, or simply enjoying a beer garden, make more noise than they realise. By the same token, since the smoking ban came into force in July 2007, there are far more people congregating outside club premises to smoke and chat. Whilst it is not suggested that either of these instances are a nuisance, they are examples of the use of the premises that the committee should be aware of. Similarly, the closing of windows and doors when amplified music or voices are being used, is another means of cutting down nuisance noise. Further advice can be obtained from the noise pollution team in the local authority.

16.5 Noise – liability towards employees for noise at work

In April 2008 the Control of Noise at Work Regulations 2005 (SI 2005/1643) (Noise Regulations) came into force for places of entertainment. The music and entertainment sectors are defined in the Noise Regulations as all workplaces where: (1) live music is played; or (2) recorded music is played in a restaurant, bar, public house, discotheque or nightclub, or alongside live music or a live dramatic or dance performance. The Noise Regulations do not apply to members of the public. When attending concerts they are making an informed choice to do so and they attend relatively infrequently when compared to workers.

Clubs fall within the ambit of the Noise Regulations if they offer musical entertainment in any of the common forms referred to above, and this further liability with respect to employees is dealt with below.

In brief, venues are expected to undertake the following course of action:

- assess the risks to employees from noise at work;

- take action to reduce the noise exposure that produces those risks;

- provide your employees with hearing protection if you cannot reduce the noise exposure enough by using other methods;

- make sure the legal limits on noise exposure are not exceeded;

- provide your employees with information, instruction and training;

- carry out health surveillance where there is a risk to health.

The Sound Advice website (www.soundadvice.info/) and *Sound Advice HSG 260* booklet (www.hse.gov.uk/pubns/books/hsg260.htm) have been published in collaboration with the Health and Safety Executive to provide information for venues on complying with the regulatory regime. They provide practical advice on controlling noise at work in the music and entertainment sectors, and identify good practice to avoid the effects of prolonged exposure to noise.

17 Health and Safety

17.1 Introduction

In addition to its duties as an occupier of premises, a club usually also has duties because of its position as an employer of staff. Every employer has a duty, under the Health and Safety at Work etc Act 1974, to ensure, so far as is reasonably practicable, the health, safety and welfare at work of all its employees. The Management of Health and Safety at Work Regulations 1999 (SI 1999/3242) also apply to every workplace and require all risks to be assessed and controlled.

If an employee has suffered an injury at work or become ill because of dangerous conditions he or she was exposed to in the workplace, he or she may seek compensation from the club. With this in mind, the Employers' Liability (Compulsory Insurance) Act 1969 requires that the employer carries a minimum insurance cover to deal with any claims arising in the workplace. The minimum level of cover at law is £5 million, although in practice most insurers offer cover of £10 million including legal costs.

17.2 Duties as an employer

Having set out the general duty, the Health and Safety at Work etc Act 1974 goes on to specify certain duties in particular:

- the duty to ensure that any plant provided is properly maintained and that systems for carrying out work are safe and do not give rise to risk to the employee's health;

- the duty to make arrangements in connection with the use, handling, storage and transport of articles and substances that will ensure the safety of staff and the absence of risk of injury to their health;

- the duty to provide proper information, instruction, training and supervision;

- the duty to maintain the employee's place of work in a safe and risk-free condition; and

- the duty to provide a safe and risk-free working environment.

To fulfil these obligations, a club employing staff may have to provide information and training in respect of the potential dangers to people other than its own employees who may work on the club premises or visit the premises from time to time. This is because the Act imposes a duty on the employer to conduct the undertaking so as to ensure, as far as is reasonably practicable, that persons not in his employment who may be affected thereby are not exposed to risks to their health and safety. The cases of *R v Swan Hunter Shipbuilders Ltd* [1982] 1 All ER 264 and *R v Board of Trustees of the Science Museum* [1993] 1 WLR 1171 are relevant. The latter case seems to suggest that in prosecutions arising from this statutory obligation, it is sufficient for the prosecution to prove that members of the public were exposed to a possibility of danger.

The legislation also embraces the responsibilities that most people would expect employees to have in safeguarding their own health and welfare. It provides that employees are under a general duty to:

- take reasonable care for their own safety and for the safety of any other person who may be affected by the employee's acts or omissions while at work; and

- co-operate with the employer as far as is necessary to enable the employer to comply with the duties under the Act.

17.3   Risk assessment

To comply with the common law duty of care and statutory obligations to those who visit or work in a club's premises, and with the club's duties to other people who may come onto those premises or may otherwise be affected by club activities, officers and committee members need to be fully aware of the nature and extent of the risks that exist at the premises. In order to demonstrate that it has understood such risk there will need to be a risk assessment. The statutory body with responsibility for overseeing health and safety matters is the Health and Safety Executive (HSE), and it describes a risk assessment as:

> A risk assessment is simply a careful examination of what, in your work, could cause harm to people, so that you can weigh up whether you have taken enough precautions or should do more to prevent harm. Workers and others have a right to be protected from harm caused by a failure to take reasonable control measures.

17.4   Advice

The HSE publishes a number of very helpful publications containing advice on a wide range of safety matters. In addition, if a club were to get into difficulties in assessing risks at its premises, the local authority health and safety inspector is responsible for small-scale commercial enterprises and will always be available to give advice.

Among the publications available from the HSE are:

- *Essentials of Health and Safety at Work*, available from the HSE website at www.hse.gov.uk/pubns/priced/essentials.pdf;

- *Management of Health and Safety at Work*, available from the HSE website at www.hse.gov.uk/pubns/priced/l21.pdf.

- *Writing your Health and Safety Policy Statement.*

The executive also supplies a number of helpful booklets containing advice expressed in straightforward language. They include:

- *An Introduction to Health and Safety*; and

- *Five Steps to Risk Assessment*, available from the HSE website at www.hse.gov.uk/pubns/indg163.pdf.

The five topics addressed in the latter booklet are:

- looking for hazards;

- deciding who might be harmed, and how;

- evaluating the risks arising from the hazards and deciding whether existing precautions are adequate;

- recording findings, and

- reviewing and revising assessments.

The following extracts give a flavour of the guidance contained in the document:

> … walk around your workplace [club premises] and look afresh at what could reasonably be expected to cause harm … Ask your employees or their representatives what they think …

> Decide who might be harmed and how. Don't forget … cleaners, visitors, contractors, maintenance contractors etc who may not be in the workplace all the time …

> What you have to decide for each significant hazard is whether the remaining risk is high, medium or low. First ask yourself whether you have done all the things that the law says you have got to do.

> In taking action ask yourself, a) can I get rid of the hazard altogether? b) if not, how can I control the risks so that harm is unlikely? …

> If you have fewer than five employees you do not need to write anything down … but if you employ five or more people you must record the

significant findings of your assessment. This means writing down the significant hazards and conclusions ...

You need to be able to show that a proper check was made, you asked who might be affected, you dealt with all the obvious significant hazards ..., the precautions are reasonable and the remaining risk is low.

The Health and Safety Executive has an information hotline: 08701 545 500. Its website address is www.hse.gov.uk.

18 Food Safety

18.1 Introduction

Clubs which sell or provide food to members and guests must be aware of their obligations under the Food Safety Act 1990 and related regulations on food hygiene. Under the 1990 Act regulations apply to the supply of food during the course of a business, otherwise than on sale, and so it follows that even the provision of sandwiches for a visiting crib team, or 'tea' for a cricket team, is regulated. The Food Standards Agency provides extensive guidance on these matters by way of website and paper documents (www.food.gov.uk) to anyone who owns, manages or works in a food business. Thus, whether clubs sell publicly or privately, in a hotel or marquee, for profit or for fund-raising, or give food away in the course of club business – the regulations bite.

Generally, anyone who handles food or whose actions could affect its safety must follow the regulations. On the basis of this advice, it is clear that any members' club that provides food must comply with the regulations. This means that they will need to register their premises as a food business with the local authority.

18.2 Food Safety Act 1990

The Food Safety Act 1990 applies to anyone who sells food for human consumption, or who offers, exposes, advertises, or is in possession of food for sale. Failure to meet its requirements is an offence. Since the Act came into force it has been amended and supplemented by a series of statutory instruments introducing new regulations. The whole of the law on food safety has now been harmonized under a series of EU regulations which are intended to govern the business of food supply from 'farm to fork'.

The Food Safety Act 1990 is to a degree a scaffold upon which have been mounted these various sets of regulation. Principally, caterers need to be aware of the General Food Regulations 2004 (SI 2004/3279) and the Food Hygiene (England) Regulations 2006 (SI 2006/14) and Food Hygiene (Wales) Regulations 2006 (SI 2006/31 (W5)), the latter of which deal with the establishment of a safe system of food preparation.

For the purposes of the Food Safety Act 1990, food is defined as 'any substance or product, whether processed, partially processed, intended to be, or reasonably expected to be ingested by humans' (Regulation (EC) 178/2002, Art 2). The definition is wide ranging and embraces everything from tea to chewing gum, pork pies to gin.

The Food Standards Agency describes the principal responsibilities under the Food Safety Act 1990 as being:

• To ensure you do not include anything in food, remove anything from food or treat food in any way which means it would be damaging to the health of people eating it.

• To ensure that the food you serve or sell is of the nature substance or quality which consumers would expect.

• To ensure that the food is labelled, advertised and presented in a way that is not false or misleading.

18.3   Offences

It is an offence under s 7 to render food injurious to health. In most cases 'rendering a food injurious to health' will apply to the manufacture of food products, but the addition of a dangerous additive or an excess of salt or sugar to food in a kitchen might trigger this offence.

It is also an offence to sell food which is not of the nature, substance or quality demanded by the purchaser (s 14). Thus where food is mis-described (eg turkey as chicken) or contains foreign bodies, or is not of the requisite standard (such as stale food, sour milk).

The maximum penalty which may be imposed in the magistrates' court, in respect of each of these offences, is a fine not exceeding £20,000, or a period of imprisonment not exceeding 6 months, or both. If a person is convicted of this offence in the Crown Court, the maximum term of imprisonment which may be imposed is 2 years. The maximum fine is four times higher than the usual maximum for a single offence, and is an indication of the seriousness of these offences.

The Act also creates an offence of falsely describing or presenting food (s 15). Great care should be taken to see that when food or drink is sold or offered for sale it is described accurately. The maximum penalty is a fine not exceeding £5,000. A club which is a corporate body may be prosecuted independently of any prosecution that may be brought against its secretary, chairman or other officer.

If a person sells food which is not of the proper nature, substance or quality, or falsely describes or presents food, because of an act or default of some other person, that other person is also guilty of an offence and may be charged with it and convicted, whether or not proceedings are taken against the first person. Consequently, if a club commits one of these offences because of an act or default by its bar steward, both the club and the bar steward may be prosecuted.

The legislation does provide for a statutory defence, although generally it is thought that the offence is one of absolute or strict liability (*Betts v Armstead* (1888) LR 20 QBD 771, *Winter v Hinckley and District Industrial Co-operative Society Ltd* [1959] 1 WLR 182 and *Goodfellow v Johnson* [1966] 1 QB 83). The defence is to prove (on the balance of probabilities) that the defendant took all reasonable precautions and exercised all due diligence to avoid committing the offence, or to avoid the commission of the offence by a person under the defendant's control.

A person charged with either of these two offences, who neither prepared the food in question nor imported it into Great Britain, establishes the statutory defence by proving:

• that the commission of the offence was due to an act or default of another person (joined in the defence) who was not under the defendant's control, or to reliance on information supplied by such a person and that the defendant carried out all such checks of the food as were reasonable in all the circumstances, or that it was reasonable to rely on checks carried out by the person who supplied the food; and

• that the defendant did not know and had no reason to suspect at the time of the alleged offence that the act or omission would amount to an offence.

This provision could be important where the food complained about was not prepared in the club but bought in from an outside supplier.

A club which intends to rely on a statutory defence as described above must serve on the prosecutor a notice in writing giving whatever information it has in its possession identifying or assisting with the identification of the other person. The notice must be given at least 7 clear days before the hearing, but where the club has previously appeared before a court in connection with the alleged offence, it must give the notice within one month of its first such appearance. The purpose of the notice is to give the prosecuting authority the opportunity to check the details given. The notice may result in the prosecution of the supplier and the withdrawal of the case against the club (*Kilhey Court Hotels Ltd V Wigan Metropolitan Borough Council* [2004] EWHC 2890 (Admin), [2005] LLR 115.

Whether or not food is unfit for human consumption is largely a question of fact in each case. The fact that a food inspector used statutory powers to condemn food is not conclusive proof that it was unfit for human consumption, although such condemnation would be strong evidence that it was (*Waye v Thompson* (1885) 15 QBD 342).

18.4   The regulations

Many regulations have been made under the Food Safety Act 1990, only some of which are relevant to retailers. Of greatest interest to clubs that sell food are the General Food Regulations 2004, and the Food Hygiene (England) Regulations 2006. These latter contain, inter alia, general requirements for food premises and specific requirements for rooms where foodstuffs are prepared (by incorporation of EU regulations in Sch II to the Regulations).

Operators now need to be aware of the requirement to operate a food safety management system based on the concept of HACCP (Hazard Analysis Critical Control Point).

This is an emergent and technical field of regulation and the reader is recommended to read the Food Standards Agency's guidance for small businesses. Whilst the Food Standards Agency is directly concerned with the observance of food hygiene and contamination issues (for instance in mass outbreaks of food poisoning), by and large the enforcement of the regulations is the responsibility of local authorities, either through the Trading Standards department, or through environmental health officers.

The provisions that relate to food premises generally include requirements concerning:

- the cleanliness of the premises;

- the design and condition of the premises;

- lavatories and washbasins; and

- hand-washing equipment.

They also deal with:

- ventilation of the premises generally;

- ventilation of sanitary conveniences;

- lighting;

- drainage; and

- changing facilities for staff.

The specific provisions concerning food preparation rooms include requirements in relation to:

- floor surfaces;

- wall surfaces;

- ceilings and overhead fixings;

- windows and other openings;

- doors;

- work surfaces;

- the cleaning of equipment; and

- the washing of food.

Some of these points are dealt with in greater detail in the paragraphs that follow.

18.5   Risk assessment

The need for clubs to carry out regular risk assessments in the context of health and safety has already been mentioned (see above). Such assessments are just as important in relation to a club's obligations under food safety legislation. Clubs operating as food businesses will be required to put in place, implement and maintain food safety management procedures based on HACCP principles – a food safety management system that focuses on 'critical points' where food safety hazards (ie microbiological, physical, chemical) could arise, and then puts in place controls and checks to prevent things going wrong.

HACCP requires a system of forward planning, staff training and documentary record-keeping. To the un-initiated there appears to be a maze of regulation, but the application of such rules is intended to be proportionate to the size of the undertaking. The environmental health departments of local authorities are responsible for monitoring establishments which sell food to ensure that food hygiene regulations are complied with, and under the 2006 Regulations all food businesses must now be registered with the local authority. Many publish their own guides to setting up a food business. A club that wishes to sell food is well advised to contact the local environmental health officer, who will be pleased to offer guidance and may be able to provide helpful literature.

When carrying out HACCP risk assessments, a club should adopt a systematic approach, focusing on potential hazards as well as hazards that are immediately obvious, every aspect of the food business and working practices, as well as working conditions. The operation should be looked at from the purchase of supplies or ingredients through to the service of food to members and guests; in respect of every point in the procedure, the question whether there is any actual or potential hazard should be posed. If any hazard is identified, the club should go on to see what controls are in place, or should be put in place, to guard against the risk(s) identified.

Some of the works that may need to be put in hand before a club could provide food safely are comparatively simple and inexpensive. In other cases, they may be substantial and costly. Clubs should consider the cost of complying with food hygiene regulations before embarking on catering for the first time. It may be that a club has to accept that it cannot undertake the sale or supply of food because of financial considerations.

18.6 The regulations in greater detail

A study of the Food Safety (England) Regulations 2006 (Food Safety (Wales) Regulations 2006 (SI 2006/31 (W.5)) shows that, when establishing an acceptable system for the preparation and handling of food, particular attention needs to be given to:

- the construction of the premises being used, their size, layout and design, to be sure that the premises are capable of accommodating the intended procedures safely. Walls and working surfaces must be easily cleaned and regularly maintained;

- the available sanitary and hand-washing facilities and their location. Separate facilities should be available to staff, and their lavatories must not give direct access to food preparation rooms. Hot and cold running water must be available and soap and suitable hand-drying facilities must be available. The staff hand-washing facilities should be separate from the facilities provided for the purpose of washing food; and

- ventilation and lighting. There has to be suitable and sufficient natural and mechanical ventilation, and mechanical systems must be accessible for cleaning and replacing filters. Adequate natural or artificial lighting must also be available.

Generally, all food storage and preparation areas, all processing and cooking equipment and utensils, all ventilation and lighting installations and all sanitary installations must be kept clean, to prevent possible contamination of the food being prepared and supplied.

Microbiological, chemical and physical hazards need to be assessed. The following are examples of these types of hazard:

- contamination caused by bacteria present in food when it is purchased, or which may get into food during preparation processes;

- contamination as a result of cleaning chemicals or materials getting into food;

- contamination as a result of pests or foreign bodies, such as dust or broken glass, getting into food while it is being stored or during the preparation processes;

- contamination by staff who are ill.

The controls which are put into place must be effective. They must eradicate the risk of harm, or at least reduce it to an acceptable level. From time to time a risk may appear to be so great that it is not practicable to eliminate it without unreasonable expense. In such a case it may be sensible to seek advice on whether the proposed operation can be changed so that the hazard is eliminated. Environmental health officers are usually prepared to give clubs the benefit of their experience on matters such as this.

18.7 Staff training

Those responsible for running a club should ensure that any controls introduced as a result of the risk assessment are properly explained to the staff employed in the preparation or service of food. Foods must be hygienically handled. Staff must be properly supervised, and be trained in food hygiene. To be effective, safeguards relating to food and stock rotation, separation of different foodstuffs to avoid cross-contamination, and cooking or reheating food, all need to be fully understood and implemented.

The training of staff is clearly important in relation to food hygiene. Courses on the subject are available, and usually lead to certificates of competence. Where in-house training would be difficult, staff should be encouraged to attend an outside course. Again, the local authority is often able to provide information about such courses. The supervisor of HCCAP must have had relevant training, although he or she can pass on experience and policy to subordinate staff in the work place.

18.7.1 Review of systems and processes

Once safe systems are in place, an officer or nominated member of the club should be allocated responsibility for keeping them under frequent review, so that the club can be sure that any food it supplies is safe for human consumption. If the way in which food is received, prepared or supplied to members changes, it may be necessary to review the systems in place.

18.8 Further information

A pack designed to assist businesses in writing a food safety system, *Safer Food, Better Business* (SFBB), has been devised by the Food Standards Agency in conjunction with caterers. The SFBB packs, or the booklets, are available free of charge from the Food Standards Agency by phoning 0845 606 0667 or emailing foodstandards@ecgroup.uk.com, or the packs and the booklets can be viewed on the Agency's website at www.food.gov.uk/aboutus/publications/safetyandhygiene.

The Department of Health publishes helpful leaflets. They include *Assured Safe Catering, A Guide to the General Food Hygiene Regulations* and *A Guide to Food Hazards and your Business*. They are written in straightforward language. Copies can be obtained from The Department of Health, PO Box 410, Wetherby, LS23 7LN.

18.9 Product substitution

Some people are not particular about brand when they order a drink. A member or guest may simply order a double scotch without expressing any preference as to the label. In such circumstances, the club is free to supply any brand of scotch it has available. But if the purchaser asks for a specific brand of any product, that brand must be supplied if at all possible. If the requested brand is not available, the bar staff should say so, and offer an alternative, which the member or guest would be free to accept or reject.

Great care is necessary to supply the correct drink. Supplying one brand when another has been ordered without telling the customer is known as 'passing off'. Trading standards officers take an interest in such occurrences and may visit the premises to obtain evidence. If satisfied that an offence has occurred, charges may be brought.

It is an offence to apply a false trade description to any product sold or offered for sale. The Trade Descriptions Act 1968 provides that 'any person who in the course of a trade or business applies a false trade description to any goods, or supplies or offers to supply any goods to which a false trade description is applied, is guilty of an offence'.

The maximum penalty for a person convicted in the magistrates' court is a fine not exceeding £5,000; if convicted in a Crown Court, the maximum penalty is an unlimited fine, or imprisonment for a term not exceeding 2 years, or both.

For the purposes of the Act, 'person' includes anybody whether it is incorporated or unincorporated; it therefore includes a members' club.

The test of whether a trade description is false is whether an ordinary man would be likely to be misled by it, see the cases of *Concentrated Foods Ltd v Champ* [1944] **KB** 342 and *Amos v Britvic Ltd* (1985) 149 JP 13.

The Trade Descriptions Act 1968 also offers a defendant the opportunity to plead a statutory defence. Thus, it is a defence if the defendant proves (on the balance of probabilities):

• that the commission of the offence was due to a mistake, or to reliance on information supplied to the defendant, or to an act or default of another person, or some accident beyond the defendant's control; and

• that the defendant took all reasonable precautions and exercised all due diligence to avoid the commission of the offence by the defendant or any person under the defendant's control.

Again, prior notice of the intention to plead this defence must be given to the prosecution, together with whatever information the defendant has about the identification of any other person whose act or default gave rise to the offence.

Where the offence charged is one of supplying or offering to supply goods to which a false trade description is applied, it is a defence to prove that the defendant did not know, and could not with reasonable diligence have ascertained, that the goods did not conform to the description applied to them.

If there is any evidence that an inexpensive product has been dispensed from a vessel bearing the name of a more expensive brand, and that the payment demanded was appropriate only to the more expensive product, the offender may be charged with obtaining a pecuniary advantage by deception, or with some other offence under the Theft Act 1968.

Of course, the great danger in buying counterfeit goods for onward supply is that there is no control of quality or provenance. In the case of alcoholic drinks counterfeiting is potentially lethal. The manufacturers are unscrupulous and unsophisticated. Counterfeit drinks often contain lethal types and levels of alcohol, colourants and other additives.

In addition to a club's duty to its members and guests to ensure they are provided with the brands requested and not with substitutes, it also has a duty to producers not to become involved with 'passing off'. Understandably, the producers of branded drinks are proud of their products and go to great lengths to see that other brews are not sold in the guise of their own. If they find that their products are being 'impersonated', they will almost certainly be prepared to go to the civil courts to obtain an injunction and an order for damages (*(1) Diageo North America Inc (2) Diageo Great Britain Ltd V (1) Intercontinental Brands (Icb) Ltd (2) Intercontinental Brands (Holdings) Ltd (3) Intercontinental Beverages (Jersey) Ltd* [2010] EWHC 172 (Pat)).

Appendices

A1 Template for Club Rules

The aims and objectives of members' clubs are diverse. It is not possible to produce a set of rules that can be adopted by all clubs. This template gives an indication of the basic rules that ought to feature in the rules of a well run members' club. Particular attention has been paid to rules that must be included if the club is to satisfy the qualification criteria set out in the Licensing Act 2003. Individual clubs will need to consider the way in which they are managed and add any additional provisions that are necessary to avoid any misunderstandings or uncertainties. The guidance is given in italic type.

RULES OF THE [insert the name or title of the club]

[insert date on which the rules became effective]

1. Name, Address, Status and Objectives

Set out the name of the club and the address of the club's premises.

If the club is affiliated to a parent association or registered as a provident or friendly society, or if it is a miners' welfare institute, set out the details of the registration, etc and state whether the club is required to observe any national rules or regulations as a consequence.

Set out the aims and objects of the club, eg the promotion of sporting fellowship, or to provide the facility for social intercourse between members.

2. Use of Club Name

Specify the club name and how it is to be used in official publications of the club, on advertisements for the club and in relation to other club business, eg on letterheads, receipts and invoices.

3. The Management of the Club

This rule should set out the fact that the club is to be managed by a management committee responsible for its day-to-day running. It should include such detail as the manner in which committee members are to be nominated and elected; whether elected officers are to be ex officio members of it; the duration of office of committee members; the responsibilities to be undertaken by the committee; the extent of its delegated powers; and whether retiring members are eligible for re-election.

The rule should also specify the frequency with which the committee is to meet; the procedures to be followed at committee meetings; how many members should be in attendance to establish a quorum; and the need to keep records that can be made available to the members. For example, the rule might specify that a third of the members should retire each year but be eligible for re-election; that in the event of a deadlock following any vote of the members, the chairman should have a deciding vote; and that minutes of the meeting are to be kept and published to the members.

Other management procedures may need to be dealt with, depending on the needs of the particular club.

4.   Finance

This rule should form the basis upon which the club's financial affairs are managed and accounted for. It should deal with the way in which banking facilities are to be set up and who should have the authority to conduct financial transactions on behalf of the club. For example, the rule might provide that the club's financial transactions should be the responsibility of the management committee but that cheques, receipts and other financial documents may be signed by the officers or any two of them.

The rules should also deal with such matters as the appointment and remuneration of auditors.

To comply with the qualifying conditions set out in the Act, the rule should require the keeping of proper, audited, books of account and specify the arrangements for informing the members about the finances of the club. Any provisions or arrangements under which property or monies of the club may be applied otherwise than for the benefit of the club as a whole, or for charitable, benevolent or political purposes, should also be set out in this rule.

5.   Officers

The rules should include specific details as to the officers the club should have; how each is to be elected or appointed; their terms of office; and the scope and extent of their duties. There may be different rules in respect of different officers. For example, a club may find it convenient to have separate rules relating to the chairman, the secretary and the treasurer.

Some clubs may need to have rules relating specifically to presidents of the club and club trustees.

6.   Membership

This rule is, perhaps, one of the most important since it is indicative of whether the club is established and conducted in good faith and, therefore, a qualifying club for the purposes of the Act. This rule should deal with the types of membership that are to be available. A separate rule or sub-rule might be drawn up for each category. For example, there may be separate provisions relating to full members, associate members, temporary members, family members and honorary members.

In each case the rules must make clear that no person may be admitted to membership, or allowed the privileges of membership, unless a period of not less than two days has elapsed between nomination or application and admission. This is a specific requirement of the Act.

These rules should make clear the rights of each class of member, especially in relation to attendance at general meetings and entitlement to vote.

Generally, all full members of a club should be entitled to attend general meetings and they should all have the right to vote. They should have equal voting rights and no one member should have a casting vote. All full members should be eligible for nomination for, and election to, office and to club committees.

7.   General Meetings

The rules should make specific provisions in relation to general meetings of the members. The frequency of such meetings should be specified and the manner in which business should be conducted at them should be spelt out. For example, the rule should make clear that any suggestion that a change should be made to rules or to the way in which the club is managed must be put before the members in the form of a resolution, and that the resolution will be passed only if it has the support of the majority of members attending the meeting.

The rule should also allow for amendment to resolutions. It should provide for the quorum needed before any business can be transacted. It should make specific provisions for calling special or extraordinary meetings of the members. For example, it might provide for the officers of the club to call such meetings and for a special meeting to be called at the request of a given number of members (perhaps 20 members or 10% of the members).

8.   Alcohol

The rules of a club which includes the sale and supply of alcohol among its licensable activities should deal with how that activity is to be controlled.

Any arrangement that has the effect of restricting the club's freedom in relation to the purchase of alcohol may be taken into account by a licensing authority when deciding whether the club is established and conducted in good faith. Care should be taken to see that the rules do not impose such a restriction on the club.

The rules should specify the hours during which intoxicating liquor may be sold or supplied, and should specify the club's authority to supply guests of members, and whether the supply is to be for consumption on or off the premises.

The rules should also make clear that there are no arrangements for any person to receive any commission, percentage or similar payment on, or with reference to, the purchase of alcohol. This is an additional provision of the Act which is designed to ensure that the club is, in truth, a members' club and not one that is run for the benefit of a proprietor.

9.   Guests

A club should have a rule that specifies whether members are to be allowed to introduce guests, and any restriction to be imposed on that right. For example, the rule might provide for the introduction of guests but state that no member may introduce more than two guests at any one time, and may not introduce the same guest more than six times in any period of 12 months. The object of such a limit is to ensure that a situation does not arise in which the number of guests present on club premises greatly exceeds the number of members present.

The rule should also make clear that while on club premises guests must behave in a proper fashion and comply with club rules. It should also make the member introducing the guest responsible for the guest's conduct while on the premises.

10. Functions for Non-members

A club may have premises which are an excellent venue for functions such as weddings, birthday celebrations or seminars. The members of the club may be content for the premises to be hired out for functions for non-members from time to time, to raise funds. Where this applies, the rules should state that the premises may be made available in such a way, and how often.

If such a power is used to too great an extent, a licensing committee may conclude that the club is not a genuine members' club and therefore ceases to be qualified for a club premises certificate.

11. Other Licensable Activities

The advent of the 2003 Act brings with it a situation in which licensable activities other than the sale and supply of alcohol are authorised by a club premises certificate. The rules of the club should now reflect the wishes of the members in respect of those activities. For example, they should state how and when entertainment is to be provided for members. The rules should also contain provisions in relation to any gaming which the club is authorised to allow under the Gaming Act 1968.

A2   Club Rules or Constitution

Name of club

Each club should carefully consider the most appropriate constitution for its particular circumstances. A basic constitution is provided below, although clubs should consider Friendly Society or Community Amateur Sports Club status (see www.cascinfo.co.uk) for tax and other financial benefits.

1.   Name

1.1   The club will be called *NAME OF CLUB* and will be affiliated to the *NAME OF GOVERNING BODY*.

2.   Aims and objectives

2.1   The aims and objectives of the club will be:

To offer coaching and competitive opportunities in (sporting, cultural, community or other principal activity)

To promote the club within the local community and.

To manage the *NAME OF FACILITY*.

To ensure a duty of care to all members of the club.

To provide all its services in a way that is fair to everyone.

To ensure that all present and future members receive fair and equal treatment.

3.   Membership

3.1   *Membership should consist of officers and members of the club.* All members will be subject to the regulations of the constitution and by joining the club will be deemed to accept these regulations and codes of practice that the club has adopted.

3.2   Members will be enrolled in one of the following categories:

full member

associate member

junior member

life member.

4.   Membership fees

4.1   Membership fees will be set annually and agreed by the Executive/Management Committee or at the Annual General Meeting. Fees will be paid: annually/monthly/weekly by subscription.

5.   Officers of the club

5.1   The officers of the club will be:

Chair

Vice Chair

Honorary Secretary

Treasurer

Fixtures Secretary

Publicity Officer

Volunteer Coordinator

Club Welfare Officer

Deputy Club Welfare Officer

Other relevant positions.

5.2   Officers will be elected annually at the Annual General Meeting.

5.3   All officers will retire each year but will be eligible for re-appointment.

6.   Committee

6.1   The club will be managed through the Management Committee consisting of: *NAMES OF OFFICER POSTS*. Only these posts will have the right to vote at meetings of the Management Committee.

6.2   The Management Committee will be convened by the Secretary of the club and held no less than *NUMBER OF MEETINGS* per year.

6.3   The quorum required for business to be agreed at Management Committee meetings will be *NUMBER*.

6.4   Committee meetings will be: *NUMBER [ACCORDING TO NUMBER OF OFFICERS IN POST]*.

6.5   The Management Committee will be responsible for adopting new policy, codes of practice and rules that affect the organisation of the club.

6.6   The Management Committee will have powers to appoint sub-committees as necessary and appoint advisers to the Management Committee as necessary to fulfil its business.

6.7   The Management Committee will be responsible for disciplinary hearings of members who infringe the club rules/regulations/constitution. The Management Committee will be responsible for taking any action of suspension or discipline following such hearings.

7.   Finance

7.1   All club monies will be banked in an account held in the name of the club.

7.2   The Club Treasurer will be responsible for the finances of the club.

7.3   The financial year of the club will end on: *DATE*.

7.4   An audited statement of annual accounts will be presented by the Treasurer at the Annual General Meeting.

7.5   Any cheques drawn against club funds should hold the signatures of the Treasurer plus up to two other officers.

8.   Annual general meetings

8.1   Notice of the Annual General Meeting (AGM) will be given by the Club Secretary. Not less than 21 clear days' notice to be given to all members.

8.2   The AGM will receive a report from officers of the Management Committee and a statement of the audited accounts.

8.3   Nominations for officers of the Management Committee will be sent to the Secretary prior to the AGM.

8.4   Elections of officers are to take place at the AGM.

8.5   All members have the right to vote at the AGM.

8.6   The quorum for AGMs will be *NUMBER [USUALLY 25% OF THE MEMBERSHIP]*.

8.7   The Management Committee has the right to call Extraordinary General Meetings (EGMs) outside the AGM. Procedures for EGMs will be the same as for the AGM.

9.   Discipline and appeals

9.1   Where applicable the procedures laid down within the *(National Body to which the Club is affiliated)* Discipline & Appeals Procedures will be adhered to.

9.2   All complaints regarding the behaviour of members should be submitted in writing to the Secretary.

9.3   The Management Committee will meet to hear complaints within 28 days of a complaint being lodged. The committee has the power to take appropriate disciplinary action up to and including suspensions and/or expulsions up to and including 6 months; fines up to and including £X.

9.4   The outcome of a disciplinary hearing should be notified in writing to the person who lodged the complaint and the member against whom the complaint was made within 14 days of the hearing.

9.5   There will be the right of appeal to the Management Committee following disciplinary action being announced. The committee should consider the appeal within 28 days of the Secretary receiving the appeal.

10.   Dissolution

10.1   A resolution to dissolve the club can only be passed at an AGM or EGM through a majority vote of the membership.

10.2   In the event of dissolution, any assets of the club that remain will become the property of *NAME OF GOVERNING BODY OR SOME OTHER CLUB WITH SIMILAR OBJECTIVES TO THOSE OF THE CLUB.*

11.   Amendments to the constitution

11.1   The constitution will only be changed through agreement by majority vote at an AGM or EGM.

12.   Declaration

12.1   *NAME OF CLUB* hereby adopts and accepts this constitution as a current operating guide regulating the actions of members.

SIGNED: DATE:

NAME:

POSITION: Club Chair

SIGNED: DATE:

NAME:

POSITION: Club Secretary

A3   Amended Guidance Issued under Section 182 of the Licensing Act 2003, October 2010

AMENDED GUIDANCE ISSUED UNDER SECTION 182 OF THE LICENSING ACT 2003

OCTOBER 2010

Presented to Parliament pursuant to Section 182 of the Licensing Act 2003

1. Introduction

THE LICENSING ACT 2003

1.1 The 2003 Act, the associated explanatory notes and any statutory instruments made under its provisions may be viewed on the OPSI website www.opsi.gov.uk. All statutory instruments may also be viewed on the DCMS website www.culture.gov.uk. The main statutory instruments are:

- The Licensing Act 2003 (Transitional provisions) Order 2005

- The Licensing Act 2003 (Personal licences) Regulations 2005

- The Licensing Act 2003 (Premises licences and club premises certificates) Regulations 2005

- The Licensing Act 2003 (Licensing authority's register) (other information) Regulations 2005

- The Licensing Act 2003 (Hearings) Regulations 2005

- The Licensing Act 2003 (Hearings) (Amendment) Regulations 2005

- The Licensing Act 2003 (Permitted Temporary Activities) (Notices) Regulations 2005

- The Licensing Act 2003 (Transitional conversions fees) Order 2005

- The Licensing Act 2003 (Fees) (Amendment) Regulations 2005

LICENSING OBJECTIVES AND AIMS

1.2 The legislation provides a clear focus on the promotion of four statutory objectives which must be addressed when licensing functions are undertaken:

The licensing objectives
- The prevention of crime and disorder.
- Public safety.
- The prevention of public nuisance.
- The protection of children from harm.

1.3 Each objective is of equal importance. It is important to note that there are no other licensing objectives, so that these four objectives are paramount considerations at all times.

1.4 But the legislation also supports a number of other key aims and purposes. These are vitally important and should be principal aims for everyone involved in licensing work. They include:

- the necessary protection of local residents, whose lives can be blighted by disturbance and anti-social behaviour associated with the behaviour of some people visiting licensed premises of entertainment;

- the introduction of better and more proportionate regulation to give business greater freedom and flexibility to meet customers' expectations;

- greater choice for consumers, including tourists, about where, when and how they spend their leisure time;

- the encouragement of more family friendly premises where younger children can be free to go with the family;

- the further development within communities of our rich culture of live music, dancing and theatre, both in rural areas and in our towns and cities; and

- the regeneration of areas that need the increased investment and employment opportunities that a thriving and safe night-time economy can bring.

11

THE GUIDANCE.

1.5 Section 182 of the Licensing Act 2003 ("the 2003 Act") provides that the Secretary of State must issue and, from time to time, may revise guidance to licensing authorities on the discharge of their functions under the 2003 Act.

Purpose

1.6 The Guidance is provided for licensing authorities carrying out their functions. It also provides information for magistrates hearing appeals against licensing decisions and has been made widely available for the benefit of operators of licensed premises, their legal advisers and the general public. It is a key mechanism for promoting best practice, ensuring consistent application of licensing powers across the country and for promoting fairness, equal treatment and proportionality.

1.7 The police remain key enforcers of licensing law. The Guidance has no binding effect on police officers who, within the terms of their force orders and the law, remain operationally independent. However, the Guidance is provided to support and assist police officers in interpreting and implementing the 2003 Act in the promotion of the four licensing objectives.

Legal status

Section 4 of the 2003 Act provides that in carrying out its functions a licensing authority must 'have regard to' guidance issued by the Secretary of State under section 182. The requirement is therefore binding on all licensing authorities to that extent.

However, the guidance cannot anticipate every possible scenario or set of circumstances that may arise and as long as licensing authorities have properly understood the Guidance they may depart from it if they have reason to do so as long as they are able to provide full reasons.

Departure from the Guidance could give rise to an appeal or judicial review, and the reasons given will then be a key consideration for the courts when considering the lawfulness and merits of any decision taken.

1.8 Nothing in this Guidance should be taken as indicating that any requirement of licensing law or any other law may be overridden (including the obligations placed on the authorities under human rights legislation). The Guidance does not in any way replace the statutory provisions of the 2003 Act or add to its scope and licensing authorities should note that interpretation of the Act is a matter for the courts. Licensing authorities and others using the Guidance must take their own professional and legal advice about its implementation.

LICENSING POLICIES

1.9   Section 5 of the Act requires a licensing authority to prepare and publish a statement of its licensing policy every three years. The policy must be published before the authority carries out any licensing function in relation to applications made under the Act.

1.10   However, making a statement is a licensing function and as such the authority must have regard to the Secretary of State's Guidance when making and publishing its policy. A licensing authority may depart from its own policy if the individual circumstances of any case merit such a decision in the interests of the promotion of the licensing objectives. But once again, it is important that they should be able to give full reasons for departing from their published statement of licensing policy. Where revisions to this Guidance are issued by the Secretary of State, there may be a period of time when the local policy statement is inconsistent with the Guidance, for example, during any consultation by the licensing authority. In these circumstances, the licensing authority should have regard, and give appropriate weight, to the Guidance and its own licensing policy statement.

LICENSABLE ACTIVITIES

1.11   For the purposes of the Act, the following are licensable activities:

Licensable activities

- The sale by retail of alcohol.
- The supply of alcohol by or on behalf of a club to, or to the order of, a member of the club.
- The provision of regulated entertainment.
- The provision of late night refreshment.

1.12   Further explanation of these terms is provided in Chapter 3.

AUTHORISATIONS

1.13   The Act provides for four different types of authorisation, as follows:

Authorisations

- Personal licences – to sell or supply alcohol and/or authorise the sale/supply.
- Premises Licences – to use a premises for licensable activities.
- Club Premises Certificates – to allow a qualifying club to engage in qualifying club activities as set out in Section 1 of the Act.
- Temporary Event Notices – to carry out licensable activities at a temporary event.

GENERAL PRINCIPLES

1.14   If an application for a premises licence or club premises certificate has been made lawfully and there have been no representations from responsible authorities or interested parties, the licensing authority must grant the application, subject only to conditions that are consistent with the operating schedule and relevant mandatory conditions.

Each application on its own merits

1.15   Each application must be considered on its own merits and any conditions attached to licences and certificates must be tailored to the individual style and characteristics of the premises and events concerned. This is essential to avoid the imposition of disproportionate and overly burdensome conditions on premises where there is no need for such conditions. Standardised conditions

13

should be avoided and indeed, may be unlawful where they cannot be shown to be necessary for the promotion of the licensing objectives in any individual case.

Avoiding duplication of other legal requirements

1.16   The licensing authority should only impose conditions on a premises licence or club premises certificate which are necessary and proportionate for the promotion of the licensing objectives. If other existing law already places certain statutory responsibilities on an employer or operator of premises, it cannot be necessary to impose the same or similar duties on the premises licence holder or club. It is only where additional and supplementary measures are necessary to promote the licensing objectives that necessary, proportionate conditions will need to be attached to a licence.

Hours of opening

1.17   The Government strongly believes that, prior to the introduction of the Licensing Act 2003, fixed and artificially early closing times (established under the Licensing Act 1964) were one of the key causes of rapid binge drinking prior to closing times; and one of the causes of disorder and disturbance when large numbers of customers were required to leave the premises simultaneously.

1.18   The aim through the promotion of the licensing objectives should be to reduce the potential for concentrations and achieve a slower dispersal of people from licensed premises through flexible opening times. Arbitrary restrictions that would undermine the principle of flexibility should therefore be avoided.

1.19   The four licensing objectives should be paramount considerations at all times and licensing authorities should always consider the individual merits of a case.

Partnership working

1.20   Licensing functions under the Act are only one means of promoting the delivery of the objectives described. They can make a substantial contribution in relation to licensed premises, but are not the panacea for all community problems.

1.21   Licensing authorities should work with all partners to deliver the licensing objectives, including responsible authorities, the licensed trade, local people and businesses, town centre managers, Crime and Disorder Reduction Partnerships, performers and local transport authorities and operators. For example, local businesses and a local authority may develop a Business Improvement District (BID), a partnership arrangement to take forward schemes that are of benefit to the community in that area, subject to the agreement of business rate payers.

1.22   The private sector, local residents and community groups in particular have an equally vital role to play in promoting the licensing objectives in partnership with public bodies. The Secretary of State strongly recommends that licensing authorities form licensing liaison groups and forums that bring together all the interested parties on a regular basis to monitor developments and propose possible solutions to any problems that may arise. The Secretary of State also recommends that licensing authorities should hold well publicised open meetings where local people and businesses can give their views on how well they feel the licensing objectives are being met.

RELATED LEGISLATION AND STRATEGIES

1.23 The Licensing Act is part of a wider Government strategy to tackle crime, disorder and anti-social behaviour and reduce alcohol harm. Licensing authorities should develop effective strategies with the police, and the other enforcement agencies as appropriate, for the management of the night-time economy. Central to this would be the enforcement of the law relating to the sales of alcohol to drunk and underage people and drunkenness or disorder on, or in the immediate vicinity of licensed premises. Targeted enforcement of this kind, in line with the recommendations in the 'Hampton' report[1] should have a positive impact on the immediate vicinity of the licensed premises concerned.

1.24 Local authorities are also empowered under section 13 of the Criminal Justice and Police Act 2001 to make 'designated public place orders' (DPPOs) to control the consumption of alcohol in a public place outside of licensed premises.

1.25 In addition there is nothing to prevent the police, licensing authorities and the hospitality industry reaching agreement about best practice in areas where problems are likely to arise.

1.26 Licensing law is not the primary mechanism for the general control of individuals once they are away from a licensed premises and therefore beyond the direct control of individual licensees or certificate holders. However, licensees and certificate holders should take reasonable steps to prevent the occurrence of crime and disorder and public nuisance immediately outside their premises,

for example on the pavement, in a beer garden, or (once the smoking ban comes into force) in a smoking shelter, where and to the extent that these matters are within their control.

1.27 In addition, when considering a new premises licence or following reviews that have identified problems with a particular premises, licensing authorities may consider imposing conditions as appropriate, such as preventing customers from taking open containers outside the premises or installing CCTV. However, any conditions imposed must not be aspirational and must be within the control of the licensee. For example, a condition may require a premises to adopt a particular dispersal policy, but a licensee cannot force customers to abide by it.

Crime and Disorder Act 1998

1.28 All local authorities must fulfil their obligations under section 17 of the Crime and Disorder Act 1998 when carrying out their functions as licensing authorities under the 2003 Act.

1.29 Section 17 is aimed at giving the vital work of crime and disorder reduction a focus across the wide range of local services and putting it at the heart of local decision-making. It places a duty on certain key authorities, including local authorities and police and fire and rescue authorities to do all they reasonably can to prevent crime and disorder in their area.

1.30 The Government believes that licensing authorities should, as a matter of good practice, involve Crime and Disorder Reduction Partnerships (CDRPs) in decision-making in order to ensure that statements of licensing policy include effective strategies that take full account of crime and disorder implications.

---

1 'Reducing administrative burdens: effective inspection and enforcement' by Philip Hampton, March 2003

Alcohol Harm Reduction Strategy

1.31 Licensing authorities should familiarise themselves with the relevant government's alcohol harm reduction strategy. In England this is *Safe. Sensible. Social. The next steps in the National Alcohol Strategy* published in June 2007 and in Wales the Welsh Assembly published *Tackling Substance Misuse in Wales: A Partnership Approach* in September 2000, which is currently being further developed. Licensing authorities should ensure that their licensing policies complement the relevant strategy, and subsequent measures, where these may help to promote one or more of the licensing objectives.

The Anti-Social Behaviour Act 2003

1.32 Licensing authorities need to be aware of new powers that will be available to local authorities under sections 40 and 41 of the Anti Social Behaviour Act 2003. The Act provides that if the noise from any licensed premises is causing a public nuisance, an authorised environmental health officer would have the power to issue a closure order effective for up to 24 hours. Under this provision, it is for the Chief Executive of the local authority to delegate their power to environmental health officers within their authority. If after receiving a closure order the premises remain open, the person responsible may upon summary conviction receive a fine of up to £20,000 or imprisonment for a term not exceeding three months, or both. This complements the police powers under Part 8 of the 2003 Act to close licensed premises for temporary periods.

Violent Crime Reduction Act 2006

1.33 The Violent Crime Reduction Act 2006 received Royal Assent on 8 November 2006. The Act introduces new measures to ensure that police and local communities have the powers they need to tackle guns, knives and alcohol-related violence. Relevant measures include:

– (from 3 May 2007) an amendment to the Licensing Act to introduce a new offence of persistently selling alcohol to children. The offence will be committed if, on three or more different occasions in a period of three consecutive months, alcohol is unlawfully sold to a minor on the same premises

– new powers for local authorities and the police to designate Alcohol Disorder Zones (ADZs) as a last resort to tackle alcohol related crime and disorder. The designation of an area as an ADZ will empower local authorities to charge licensees for additional enforcement activity affecting all licensed premises within the zone. The earliest date for commencement of ADZs is 1 October 2007. On commencement, relevant guidance and regulations will be placed on the Home Office website (www.homeoffice.gov.uk).

– an amendment to the Licensing Act which will enable licensing authorities, on the application of a senior police officer in cases of serious crime and disorder, to attach interim conditions to licences pending a full review. The earliest date for commencement of these powers is 1 October 2007.

LACORS Practical Guide to Test Purchasing

1.34   Licensing authorities should also familiarise themselves with the LACORS Practical Guide to Test Purchasing insofar as it relates to the test purchasing of alcohol by trading standards officers. LACORS continues to fulfil an important co-ordinating role in advising and informing licensing authorities about the requirements of the 2003 Act. LACORS' website may be viewed at www.lacors.gov.uk.

1.35   Details of other relevant industry initiatives can be found at Annex E.

The Health Act 2006 – workplace smoking ban

1.36   The ban on smoking in all enclosed workplaces and public spaces will come into force on 1 July 2007. The ban will include smoking in pubs, restaurants and members' clubs where bar or other staff are employed. In this context 'enclosed' will mean anywhere with more than 50% of wall and ceiling space infilled.

The Clean Neighbourhoods and Environment Act 2005

1.37   This provides local authorities with an additional power to issue a fixed penalty notice to any licensed premises emitting noise that exceeds the permitted level between the hours of 11pm and 7am.

The EU Services Directive

1.38   The EU Services Directive is a flagship European Directive intended to develop the single market for services by breaking down barriers to cross border trade within the EU and making it easier for service providers within scope to set up business or offer their services in other EU countries. The Directive requires that all notices and authorisations in scope are able to be completed electronically and via a 'point of single contact'. The Directive was implemented in the UK on 28 December by the Provision of Services Regulations 2009. The UK point of single contact is the Electronic Application Facility (EAF) which is part of the www.businesslink.gov website ('businesslink')

1.39   Although only regulated entertainment is a 'service' as defined under the Directive, the Government has extended the electronic application process to all regulated activities under the 2003 Act and to all authorisations and notices with the exception of applications for, and renewals of, personal licences, reviews and representations. Guidance on the new electronic application process is provided in paragraphs 8.27 – 8.35 and in relevant chapters.

Policing and Crime Act 2009

1.40   The Policing and Crime Act 2009 clarifies how police forces and local authorities can work together by placing an explicit duty on police authorities to reflect their community's priorities in their work. The 2009 Act introduced a number of measures which are relevant, or made changes, to the 2003 Act, including:

- a mandatory code of practice for alcohol retailers;
- elected members of licensing authorities included as interested parties;
- reclassification of lap dancing clubs so they require a sex establishment licence

2. The licensing objectives

CRIME AND DISORDER

2.1 The steps any licence holder or club might take to prevent crime and disorder are as varied as the premises or clubs where licensable activities may be carried on. Licensing authorities should therefore look to the police as the main source of advice on these matters. They should also seek to involve the local CDRP, as recommended in paragraph 1.21 of this Guidance.

2.2 The Government's expectation is that the police will have a key role in undertaking the following tasks:

- developing a constructive working relationship with licensing authority licensing officers and bodies such as the local authority social services department, the Area Child Protection Committee or another competent body;
- developing a constructive working relationship with designated premises supervisors and other managers of premises, including premises providing late night refreshment;
- advising, where necessary, on the development of a venue drug policy;
- developing a constructive working relationship with the Security Industry Authority including joint visits and enforcement action where appropriate;
- agreeing the protocols for actions taken by door supervisors in relation to illegal drugs or violent behaviour, particularly when police officers should be called immediately;
- advising on and approving search procedures and the storage procedures for confiscated drugs;
- gathering and sharing intelligence on drug dealing and use with partner organisations and local venues;

- advising on the installation and monitoring of security devices such as CCTV;
- advising on the provision of safe and accessible transport home in consultation with community safety colleagues, local transport authorities and transport operators;
- working with venue owners and managers to resolve drug-related problems and problems of disorder, drunkenness and anti-social behaviour; and
- advising on the protection of employees on licensed premises who may be targets for attacks and reprisals.

2.3 The Security Industry Authority also plays an important role in preventing crime and disorder by ensuring that door supervisors are properly licensed and, in partnership with police and other agencies, that security companies are not being used as fronts for serious and organised criminal activity and that door supervisors are properly licensed. This may include making specific enquiries or visiting premises through intelligence led operations in conjunction with the police, local authorities and other partner agencies. In the exercise of their functions licensing authorities should seek to co-operate with the SIA as far as possible and consider adding relevant conditions to licences where necessary and appropriate.

2.4 The essential purpose of the licence or certificate in this context is to regulate behaviour on premises and access to them where this relates to licensable activities and the licensing objectives. Conditions attached to licences cannot seek to manage the behaviour of customers once they are beyond the direct management of the licence holder and their staff or agents, but can directly impact on the behaviour of customers on, or in the immediate vicinity of, the premises as they seek to enter or leave.

2.5 Licence conditions should not replicate licensing offences that are set out in the 2003 Act. For example, a condition that states that a licence holder shall not permit drunkenness and disorderly behaviour on his premises would be superfluous because this is already a criminal offence. A condition that states that a licence holder shall not permit the sale of controlled drugs on the premises would be similarly superfluous.

2.6 Conditions are best targeted on deterrence and preventing crime and disorder. For example, where there is good reason to suppose that disorder may take place, the presence of closed-circuit television cameras both inside and immediately outside the premises can actively deter disorder, nuisance and anti-social behaviour and crime generally. Some licensees may wish to have cameras on their premises for the protection of their own staff and for the prevention of crime directed against the business itself or its customers. But any condition may require a broader approach, and it may be necessary to ensure that the precise location of cameras is set out on plans to ensure that certain areas are properly covered and there is no subsequent dispute over the terms of the condition.

2.7 Similarly, the provision of requirements for door supervision may be necessary to ensure that people who are drunk or drug dealers or carrying firearms do not enter the premises, reducing the potential for crime and disorder, and that the police are kept informed.

2.8 Text and radio pagers allow premises licence holders, designated premises supervisors and managers of premises and clubs to communicate instantly with the local police and facilitate a rapid response to any disorder which may be endangering the customers and staff on the premises. The Secretary of State recommends that text or radio pagers should be considered appropriate necessary conditions for public houses, bars and nightclubs operating in city and town centre leisure areas with a high density of licensed premises.

2.9 Some conditions primarily focused on the prevention of crime and disorder will also promote other licensing objectives. For example, a condition requiring that all glasses used on the premises for the sale of alcoholic drinks should be made of plastic or toughened glass or not allowing bottles to pass across a bar may be necessary to prevent violence by denying assailants suitable weapons, but may also benefit public safety by minimising the injury done to victims when such assaults take place (for example, facial injuries resulting from broken glass).

2.10 A condition must also be capable of being met. For example, while beer glasses may be available in toughened glass, wine glasses may not. Licensing authorities should carefully consider conditions of this kind to ensure that they are not only necessary but both practical and achievable.

2.11 Similarly, although most commonly made a condition of a licence on public safety grounds, licensing authorities should also consider conditions which set capacity limits for licensed premises or clubs where it may be necessary to prevent overcrowding likely to lead to disorder and violence. If such a condition is considered necessary, the licensing authority should consider whether door supervisors are needed to control numbers.

2.12 In the context of crime and disorder and public safety, the preservation of order on premises may give rise to genuine concerns about the competency of the management team charged with the maintenance of order. This may occur, for example, on premises where there are very large numbers of people and alcohol is supplied for consumption, or in premises where there are public order problems.

2.13 The designated premises supervisor is the key person who will usually be charged with day to day management of the premises by the premises licence holder, including the prevention of disorder. However, conditions relating to the management competency of designated premises supervisors should not normally be attached to premises licences. A condition of this kind could only be justified as necessary in rare circumstances where it could be demonstrated that in the circumstances associated with particular premises, poor management competency could give rise to issues of crime and disorder and public safety.

2.14 It will normally be the responsibility of the premises licence holder as an employer, and not the licensing authority, to ensure that the managers appointed at the premises are competent and appropriately trained and licensing authorities must ensure that they do not stray outside their powers and duties under the 2003 Act. This is important to ensure the portability of the personal licence and the offences set out in the 2003 Act ensure, for example, that the prevention of disorder is in sharp focus for all such managers, licence holders and clubs.

2.15 Communications between the managers of the premises and the police can also be crucial in preventing crime and disorder. Involvement by operators and managers in voluntary schemes and initiatives may be particularly valuable. Conditions requiring dedicated text or pager links between management teams and local police stations can provide early warning of disorder and also can be used to inform other licence holders that a problem has arisen in the area generally. For example, where a gang of youths is causing problems in one public house and their eviction will only result in them going on elsewhere to cause problems on other premises, there is advantage in communication links between the police and other licensed premises and clubs.

2.16 However, while this may be necessary and effective in certain parts of licensing authority areas, it may be less effective or even unnecessary in others. Police views on such matters should be given considerable weight and licensing authorities must remember that only necessary conditions, which are within the control of the licence holder or club, may be imposed.

2.17 The Indecent Displays Act 1981 prohibits the public display of indecent matter, subject to certain exceptions. It should not therefore be necessary for any conditions to be attached to licences or certificates concerning such displays in or outside the premises involved. For example, the display of advertising material on or immediately outside such premises is regulated by this legislation. Similarly, while conditions relating to public safety in respect of dancing may be necessary in certain

200   *Club Law Manual*

circumstances, the laws governing indecency and obscenity are adequate to control adult entertainment involving striptease and lap-dancing which goes beyond what is lawful. Accordingly, conditions relating to the content of such entertainment which have no relevance to crime and disorder, public safety, public nuisance or the protection of children from harm could not be justified. In this context, however, it should be noted that it is in order for conditions relating to the exclusion of minors or the safety of performers to be included in premises licence or club premises certificate conditions where necessary. The Local Government (Miscellaneous Provisions) Act 1982 insofar as its adoptive provisions relate to sex establishments – sex shops, sex cinemas and in London sex encounter establishments – also remains in force.

2.18   Guidance to the police on powers to close premises (formerly Chapter 11 of this Guidance) can now be found on the DCMS website at www.culture.gov.uk.

PUBLIC SAFETY

2.19   Licensing authorities and responsible authorities should note that the public safety objective is concerned with the physical safety of the people using the relevant premises and not with public health, which is dealt with in other legislation. There will of course be occasions when a public safety condition could incidentally benefit health, but it should not be the purpose of the condition as this would be ultra vires the 2003 Act. Accordingly, conditions should not be imposed on a premises licence or club premises certificate which relate to cleanliness or hygiene.

2.20   From 1 October 2006 the Regulatory Reform (Fire Safety) Order 2005 ('the Fire Safety Order') replaced previous fire safety legislation. As such any fire certificate issued under the Fire Precautions Act 1971 will have ceased to have effect. Licensing authorities should note that under article 43 of the Fire Safety Order any conditions imposed by the licensing authority that relate to any requirements or prohibitions that are or could be imposed by the Order automatically cease to have effect, without the need to vary the licence. This means that licensing authorities should not seek to impose fire safety conditions where the Order applies.

2.21   The exception to this will be in cases where the licensing authority and the enforcing authority for the fire safety order are one and the same body. For example, designated sports-grounds and stands where local authorities enforce the fire safety order. In such circumstances fire safety conditions should not be set in new licences, but conditions in existing licences will remain in force and be enforceable by the licensing authority.

2.22   The Fire Safety Order applies in England and Wales. It covers 'general fire precautions' and other fire safety duties which are needed to protect 'relevant persons' in case of fire in and around 'most premises'. The Order requires fire precautions to be put in place 'where necessary' and to the extent that it is reasonable and practicable in the circumstances of the case.

2.23   Responsibility for complying with the Order rests with the 'responsible person', which may be the employer, or any other person or people who may have control of the premises. Each responsible person must carry out a fire risk

21

assessment which must focus on the safety in case of fire for all 'relevant persons'. The fire risk assessment is intended to identify risks that can be removed or reduced and to decide the nature and extent of the general fire precautions that need to be taken including, where necessary, capacity limits.

2.24 The local fire and rescue authority will enforce the Order in most premises and have the power to inspect the premises to check the responsible person is complying with their duties under the Order. They will look for evidence that the responsible person has carried out a suitable fire risk assessment and acted upon the significant findings of that assessment. If the enforcing authority is dissatisfied with the outcome of a fire risk assessment or the action taken, they may issue an enforcement notice that requires the responsible person to make certain improvements or, in extreme cases, issue a prohibition notice that restricts the use of all or part of the premises until improvements are made.

2.25 Further information and guidance about the Order and fire safety legislation is available from the Communities and Local Government website www.communities.gov.uk/fire.

2.26 Where there is a requirement in other legislation for premises open to the public or for employers to possess certificates attesting to the safety or satisfactory nature of certain equipment or fixtures on the premises, it would be unnecessary for a licensing condition to require possession of such a certificate. However, it would be permissible to require as a condition of a licence or certificate, if necessary, checks on this equipment to be conducted at specified intervals and for evidence of these checks to be retained by the premises licence holder or club provided this does not duplicate or gold-plate a requirement in other legislation. Similarly, it would be permissible for licensing authorities, if they receive relevant representations from responsible authorities or interested parties, to attach conditions which require equipment of particular standards to be maintained on the premises. Responsible authorities – such as health and safety authorities – should therefore make clear their expectations in this respects to enable prospective licence holders or clubs to prepare effective operating schedules and club operating schedules.

2.27 "Safe capacities" should only be imposed where necessary for the promotion of public safety or the prevention of disorder on the relevant premises. For example, if a capacity has been imposed through other legislation, it would be unnecessary to reproduce it in a premises licence. Indeed, it would also be wrong to lay down conditions which conflict with other legal requirements. However, if no safe capacity has been imposed through other legislation, a responsible authority may consider it necessary for a new capacity to be attached to the premises which would apply at any material time when the licensable activities are taking place and make representations to that effect. For example, in certain circumstances, capacity limits may be necessary in preventing disorder, as overcrowded venues can increase the risks of crowds becoming frustrated and hostile.

2.28 As noted above, a capacity limit should not be imposed as a condition of the licence on fire safety grounds (unless the licensing authority and the enforcing authority for fire safety purposes are the same) since, under article 43 of the Fire Safety Order, it would have no effect and so would not be enforceable.

22

2.29   The special provisions made for dancing, amplified and unamplified music in section 177 of the 2003 Act apply only to premises with a "permitted capacity" of not more than 200 persons. In this context, the capacity must be where the fire and rescue authority has made a recommendation on the capacity of the premises under the Fire Safety Order. For any application for a premises licence or club premises certificate for premises without an existing permitted capacity where the applicant wishes to take advantage of the special provisions set out in section 177 of the 2003 Act, the applicant should conduct their own risk assessment as to the appropriate capacity of the premises. They should send their recommendation to the fire and rescue authority who will consider it and then decide what the "permitted capacity" of those premises should be.

2.30   Whilst the Cinematograph (Safety) Regulations 1955 (S.I 1995/1129) which contained a significant number of regulations in respect of fire safety provision at cinemas, no longer apply, applicants taking advantage of the "grandfather rights" pursuant to Schedule 8 to the 2003 Act will have been subject to conditions which re-state those regulations in their new premises licence or club premises certificate. Any holders of a converted licence seeking to remove these conditions and reduce the regulatory burden on them (to the extent to which that can be done while still promoting the licensing objectives), would need to apply to vary their converted licences or certificates. When considering variation applications or applications for new licences, licensing authorities and responsible authorities should recognise the need for steps to be taken to assure public safety at these premises in the absence of the 1995 Regulations.

2.31   Public safety includes the safety of performers appearing at any premises.

PUBLIC NUISANCE

2.32   The 2003 Act requires licensing authorities (following receipt of relevant representations) and responsible authorities, through representations, to make judgements about what constitutes public nuisance and what is necessary to prevent it in terms of conditions attached to specific premises licences and club premises certificates. It is therefore important that in considering the promotion of this licensing objective, licensing authorities and responsible authorities focus on impacts of the licensable activities at the specific premises on persons living and working (including doing business) in the vicinity that are disproportionate and unreasonable. The issues will mainly concern noise nuisance, light pollution, noxious smells and litter.

2.33   Public nuisance is given a statutory meaning in many pieces of legislation. It is however not narrowly defined in the 2003 Act and retains its broad common law meaning. It is important to remember that the prevention of public nuisance could therefore include low-level nuisance perhaps affecting a few people living locally as well as major disturbance affecting the whole community. It may also include in appropriate circumstances the reduction of the living and working amenity and environment of interested parties (as defined in the 2003 Act) in the vicinity of licensed premises.[2]

2.34   Conditions relating to noise nuisance will normally concern steps necessary to control the levels of noise emanating from premises. This might be achieved by a simple measure such as ensuring that doors and windows are

---

2 It should also be noted in this context that it remains an offence under the 2003 Act to sell or supply alcohol to a person who is drunk. This is particularly important because of the nuisance and anti-social behaviour which can be provoked after leaving licensed premises.

23

kept closed after a particular time in the evening to more sophisticated measures like the installation of acoustic curtains or rubber speaker mounts. Any conditions necessary to promote the prevention of public nuisance should be tailored to the style and characteristics of the specific premises. Licensing authorities should be aware of the need to avoid unnecessary or disproportionate measures that could deter events that are valuable to the community, such as live music. Noise limiters, for example, are very expensive to purchase and install and are likely to be a considerable burden for smaller venues.

2.35 As with all conditions, it will be clear that conditions relating to noise nuisance may not be necessary in certain circumstances where the provisions of the Environmental Protection Act 1990, the Noise Act 1996, or the Clean Neighbourhoods and Environment Act 2005 adequately protect those living in the vicinity of the premises. But as stated earlier in this Guidance, the approach of licensing authorities and responsible authorities should be one of prevention and when their powers are engaged, licensing authorities should be aware of the fact that other legislation may not adequately cover concerns raised in relevant representations and additional conditions may be necessary.

2.36 Where applications have given rise to representations, any necessary and appropriate conditions should normally focus on the most sensitive periods. For example, music noise from premises usually occurs from mid-evening until either late evening or early morning when residents in adjacent properties may be attempting to go to sleep or are sleeping. In certain circumstances, conditions

relating to noise in the immediate vicinity of the premises may also prove necessary to address any disturbance anticipated as customers enter and leave.

2.37 Measures to control light pollution will also require careful thought. Bright lighting outside premises considered necessary to prevent crime and disorder may itself give rise to light pollution for some neighbours. Applicants, licensing authorities and responsible authorities will need to balance these issues.

2.38 In the context of preventing public nuisance, it is again essential that conditions are focused on measures within the direct control of the licence holder or club. Conditions relating to public nuisance caused by the anti-social behaviour of customers once they are beyond the control of the licence holder, club or premises management cannot be justified and will not serve to promote the licensing objectives.

2.39 Beyond the vicinity of the premises, these are matters for personal responsibility of individuals under the law. An individual who engages in anti-social behaviour is accountable in their own right. However, it would be perfectly reasonable for a licensing authority to impose a condition, following relevant representations, that requires the licence holder or club to place signs at the exits from the building encouraging patrons to be quiet until they leave the area and to respect the rights of people living nearby to a peaceful night.

2.40 The cumulative effects of litter in the vicinity of premises carrying on licensable activities can cause public nuisance. For example, it may be appropriate and necessary for a condition of a licence to require premises serving customers from take-aways and fast food outlets from 11.00pm to provide litter bins in the vicinity of the premises in order to prevent the accumulation of litter. Such conditions may be necessary and appropriate in circumstances where customers late at night may have been consuming alcohol and be inclined to carelessness and anti-social behaviour.

PROTECTION OF CHILDREN FROM HARM

2.41 The protection of children from harm includes the protection of children from moral, psychological and physical harm, and this would include the protection of children from too early an exposure to strong language and sexual expletives, for example, in the context of film exhibitions or where adult entertainment is provided.

2.42 However, in the context of many licensed premises such as pubs, restaurants, café bars and hotels, it should be noted that the Secretary of State recommends that the development of family-friendly environments should not be frustrated by overly restrictive conditions in relation to children.

2.43 The Secretary of State intends that the admission of children to premises holding a premises licence or club premises certificate should normally be freely allowed without restricting conditions unless the 2003 Act itself imposes such a restriction or there are good reasons to restrict entry or to exclude children completely. Licensing authorities, the police and other authorised persons should focus on enforcing the law concerning the consumption of alcohol by minors.

2.44 Conditions relating to the access of children which are necessary to protect them from harm are self evidently of great importance. As mentioned in connection with statements of licensing policy in Chapter 13 of this Guidance, issues will arise about the access of children in connection with premises:

- where adult entertainment is provided;
- where a member or members of the current management have been convicted for serving alcohol to minors or with a reputation for allowing underage drinking (other than in the context of the exemption in the 2003 Act relating to 16 and 17 year olds consuming beer, wine and cider in the company of adults during a table meal);
- where it is known that unaccompanied children have been allowed access;
- where requirements for proof of age cards or other age identification to combat the purchase of alcohol by minors is not the norm;
- with a known association with drug taking or dealing;
- where there is a strong element of gambling on the premises (but not small numbers of cash prize machines);
- where the supply of alcohol for consumption on the premises is the exclusive or primary purpose of the services provided at the premises.

2.45 It is also possible that activities, such as adult entertainment, may take place at certain times on premises but not at other times. For example, premises may operate as a café bar during the day providing meals for families but also provide entertainment with a sexual content after 8.00pm. Such trading practices should be obvious from the operating schedule or club operating schedule provided with the relevant application allowing the framing of an appropriate, time-limited condition.

25

2.46 Similarly, gambling may take place in part of a leisure centre but not in other parts of those premises. This means that the access of children will need to be carefully considered by applicants, licensing authorities and responsible authorities. In many respects, it should be possible to rely on the discretion and common sense of licence and certificate holders. However, licensing authorities and responsible authorities should still expect applicants when preparing an operating schedule or club operating schedule to state their intention to exercise discretion and where they are necessary, to set out the steps to be taken to protect children from harm when on the premises.

2.47 Conditions, where they are necessary, should reflect the licensable activities taking place on the premises and can include:

- where alcohol is sold, requirements for the production of proof of age cards or other age identification before sales are made, to ensure that sales are not made to individuals under 18 years (whether the age limit is 18 or 16 as in the case of the consumption of beer, wine and cider in the company of adults during a table meal);

- restrictions on the hours when children may be present;

- restrictions on the presence of children under certain ages when particular specified activities are taking place;

- restrictions on the parts of the premises to which children may have access;

- age restrictions (below 18);

- restrictions or exclusions when certain activities are taking place;

- requirements for accompanying adult (including for example, a combination of requirements which provide that children under a particular age must be accompanied by an adult); and

- full exclusion of people under 18 from the premises when any licensable activities are taking place

2.48 The Secretary of State considers that representations made by the child protection bodies and the police in respect of individual applications should be given considerable weight when they address necessary issues regarding the admission of children.

2.49 The 2003 Act provides that where a premises licence or club premises certificate authorises the exhibition of a film, it must include a condition requiring the admission of children to films to be restricted in accordance with recommendations given either by a body designated under section 4 of the Video Recordings Act 1984 specified in the licence (the British Board of Film Classification is currently the only body which has been so designated) or by the licensing authority itself. Further details are given in Chapter 10.

2.50 The admission of children to theatres, as with other licensed premises, should not normally be restricted. However, theatres may present a range of diverse activities. The admission of children to the performance of a play should normally be at the discretion of the licence holder and no condition restricting their access to plays should be attached. However, theatres may also present a wide range of entertainment including, for example, variety shows incorporating adult entertainment. A condition restricting the admission of children in such circumstances may be necessary. Entertainments may also be presented at theatres specifically for children. It may be necessary to consider whether a condition

should be attached to a premises licence or
club premises certificate which requires the
presence of a sufficient number of adult staff
on the premises to ensure the well being of the
children during any emergency.

Offences relating to the sale and supply of alcohol to children

2.51 Licensing authorities are expected to maintain
close contact with the police, young offenders'
teams and trading standards officers (who can
carry out test purchases under s.154 of the
Act) about the extent of unlawful sales and
consumption of alcohol by minors and to be
involved in the development of any strategies
to control or prevent these unlawful activities
and to pursue prosecutions. For example,
where as a matter of policy, warnings are given
to retailers prior to any decision to prosecute
in respect of an offence, it is important that
each of the enforcement arms should be aware
of the warnings each of them has given.

Table of relevant offences under the 2003 Act

Section	Offence
Section 145	Unaccompanied children prohibited from certain premises
Section 146	Sale of alcohol to children
Section 147	Allowing the sale of alcohol to children
Section 147A	Persistently selling alcohol to children
Section 148	Sale of liqueur confectionery to children under 16
Section 149	Purchase of alcohol by or on behalf of children
Section 150	Consumption of alcohol by children
Section 151	Delivering alcohol to children
Section 152	Sending a child to obtain alcohol
Section 153	Prohibition of unsupervised sales by children

6. Club premises certificates

6.1   This Chapter provides advice about best practice for the administration of the processes for issuing, varying, and reviewing club premises certificates and other associated procedures.

GENERAL

6.2   Clubs are organisations where members have joined together for particular social, sporting or political purposes and then combined to buy alcohol in bulk as members of the organisation to supply in the club. They commonly include Labour, Conservative and Liberal Clubs, the Royal British Legion, other ex-services clubs, working men's clubs, miners welfare institutions, social and sports clubs.

6.3   Technically the club only sells alcohol by retail at such premises to guests. Where members purchase alcohol, there is no sale (as the member owns part of the alcohol stock) and the money passing across the bar is merely a mechanism to preserve equity between members where one may consume more than another. This explains why the 2003 Act often refers to the supply of alcohol in the context of clubs and not just to the sale by retail.

6.4   Only 'qualifying' clubs may hold club premises certificates. In order to be a qualifying club, a club must have at least 25 members and meet the conditions set out in paragraph 6.9 below. The grant of a club premises certificate means that a qualifying club is entitled to certain benefits. These include:

  · the authority to supply alcohol to members and sell it to guests on the premises to which the certificate relates without the need for any member or employee to hold a personal licence;

  · the absence of a requirement to specify a designated premises supervisor (see paragraphs 4.19 and 4.20 of this Guidance);

  · more limited rights of entry for the police and authorised persons because the premises are considered private and not generally open to the public;

  · exemption from police powers of instant closure on grounds of disorder and noise nuisance (except when being used under the authority of a temporary event notice or premises licence) because they operate under their codes of discipline and rules which are rigorously enforced ; and

  · exemption from orders of the magistrates' court for the closure of all licensed premises in an area when disorder is happening or expected.

6.5   Qualifying clubs should not be confused with proprietary clubs, which are clubs run commercially by individuals, partnerships or businesses for profit. These require a premises licence and are not qualifying clubs.

6.6   A qualifying club will be permitted under the terms of a club premises certificate to sell and supply alcohol to its members and their guests only. Instant membership is not permitted and members must wait at least two days between their application and their admission to the club. Any qualifying club may choose to obtain a premises licence if it decides that it wishes to offer its facilities commercially for use by the general public, including the sale of alcohol to them. However, an individual on behalf of a club may give temporary event notices in respect of the premises to cover a period of up to 96 hours on up to 12 occasions each calendar year, so long as no more than 499 people attend the event and subject to an overall maximum duration in the year of 15 days, and on such occasions may sell alcohol to the public or hire out their premises for use by the public.

6.7   The 2003 Act does not prevent visitors to a qualifying club being supplied with alcohol as long as they are 'guests' of any member of the club or the club collectively, and nothing in the 2003 Act prevents the admission of such people as guests without prior notice. For the sake of flexibility, the Act does not define "guest" and whether or not somebody is a genuine guest would in all cases be a question of fact. The term can include a wide variety of people who are invited by the qualifying club or any individual member to use the club facilities. The manner in which they are admitted as 'guests' would be for the club to determine and to consider setting out in their own club rules.

6.8   There is no mandatory requirement under the 2003 Act for guests to be signed in by a member of the club. However, a point may be reached where a club is providing commercial services to the general public in a way that is contrary to its qualifying club status. It is at this point that the club would no longer be conducted in "good faith" and would no longer meet "general condition 3" for qualifying clubs in section 62 of the 2003 Act . Under the 2003 Act the licensing authority must decide when a club has ceased to operate in "good faith" and give the club a notice withdrawing the club premises certificate. The club is entitled to appeal against such a decision to the magistrates' courts. Unless the appeal is successful, the club would need to apply for a full premises licence to cover any licensable activities taking place there.

QUALIFYING CONDITIONS

6.9   Section 62 of the 2003 Act sets out five general conditions which a relevant club must meet to be a qualifying club. Section 63 also sets out specified matters for licensing authorities to enable them to determine whether a club is established and conducted in good faith – the third qualifying condition. Section 64 sets out additional conditions which only need to be met by clubs intending to supply alcohol to members and guests. Section 90 of the 2003 Act gives powers to the licensing authority to issue a notice to a club withdrawing its certificate where it appears that it has ceased to meet the qualifying conditions. There is a right of appeal against such a decision.

ASSOCIATE MEMBERS AND GUESTS

6.10   As well as their own members and guests, qualifying clubs are also able to admit associate members and their guests (i.e. members and guests from another 'recognised club' as defined by section 193 of the 2003 Act) to the club premises when qualifying club activities are being carried on without compromising the use of their club premises certificate. This reflects traditional arrangements where such clubs make their facilities open to members of other clubs which operate reciprocal arrangements.

APPLICATIONS FOR THE GRANT OR VARIATION OF CLUB PREMISES CERTIFICATES

6.11 The arrangements for applying for or seeking to vary club premises certificates are extremely similar to those for a premises licence. Clubs may also use the minor variation process to make small changes to their certificates as long as these could have no adverse impact on the licensing objectives. Licensing authorities should refer to Chapter 8 of this Guidance on the handling of such applications. In that Chapter most of the references to the premises licence, premises licence holders, and applicants can be read for the purposes of this Chapter as club premises certificates, qualifying clubs and club applicants.

6.12 In addition to a plan of the premises and a club operating schedule, clubs must also include the rules of the club with their application. On notifying any alteration to these rules to the licensing authority, the club is required to pay a fee set down in regulations. Licensing authorities may wish to consider returning a certified copy of the rules to the applicant with the certificate. Licensing authorities should bear in mind that they cannot require any changes to the rules to be made as a condition of receiving a certificate unless relevant representations have been made. However, if a licensing authority is satisfied that the rules of a club indicate that it does not meet the qualifying conditions in the Act, a club premises certificate should not be granted.

STEPS NEEDED TO PROMOTE THE LICENSING OBJECTIVES

6.13 Club operating schedules prepared by clubs, as with operating schedules for premises licences, must include the steps the club intends to take to promote the licensing objectives. These will be translated into conditions included in the certificate, unless the conditions have been modified by the licensing authority following consideration of relevant representations. Guidance on these conditions is given in Chapter 10 of this Guidance.

6.14 The Secretary of State wishes to emphasise that non-profit making clubs make an important and traditional contribution to the life of many communities in England and Wales and bring significant benefits. Their activities also take place on premises to which the public do not generally have access and they operate under codes of discipline applying to members and their guests.

6.15 Licensing authorities should bear these matters in mind when considering representations and should not attach conditions to certificates unless they can be demonstrated to be strictly necessary. The indirect costs of conditions will be borne by individual members of the club and cannot be recovered by passing on these costs to the general public.

SEX EQUALITY

6.16 The Secretary of State believes that all qualifying clubs should adopt fair and equal procedures for admitting people to membership, electing club officials and on voting rights. However, although equal treatment on the grounds of gender is important to society generally, it is not a licensing objective. Conditions should not therefore be imposed which interfere with the arrangements for granting membership or voting within the club. It would also be inappropriate to apply one set of rules to qualifying clubs and another set of rules to clubs that do not engage in qualifying club activities and do not therefore require club premises certificates. Licensing authorities should not therefore seek to challenge the bona fides of any qualifying club on these grounds.

TEMPORARY EVENT NOTICES

6.17 Licensing authorities should note paragraph 7.13 of this Guidance in connection with permitted temporary activities in club premises.

10. Conditions attached to premises licences and club premises certificates

GENERAL

10.1 This chapter provides advice and recommendations concerning best practice in relation to conditions attached to premises licences and club premises certificates.

10.2 Conditions include any limitations or restrictions attached to a licence or certificate and essentially are the steps or actions the holder of the premises licence or the club premises certificate will be required to take or refrain from taking at all times when licensable activities are taking place at the premises in question.

10.3 All interests – licensing authorities, licence and certificate holders, authorised persons, the police, other responsible authorities and local residents and businesses – should be working together in partnership to ensure collectively that the licensing objectives are promoted.

10.4 Under former licensing regimes, the courts have made clear that it is particularly important that conditions which are imprecise or difficult for a licence holder to observe should be avoided. Failure to comply with any conditions attached to a licence or certificate is a criminal offence, which on conviction would be punishable by a fine of up to £20,000 or up to six months imprisonment or both.

10.5 Annex D provides pools of conditions (although not an exhaustive list) which relate to the four licensing objectives and could be used where necessary and appropriate to the particular circumstances of an individual licensed premises. It is important that they should not be applied universally and treated as standard conditions irrespective of circumstances.

10.6 There are three types of condition that may be attached to a licence or certificate: proposed, imposed and mandatory. Each of these categories is described in more detail below.

PROPOSED CONDITIONS

10.7 The conditions that are necessary for the promotion of the licensing objectives should emerge initially from a prospective licensee's or certificate holder's risk assessment which applicants and clubs should carry out before making their application for a premises licence or club premises certificate. This would be translated into the steps recorded in the operating schedule or club operating schedule which must also set out the proposed hours of opening.

10.8 In order to minimise problems and the necessity for hearings, it would be sensible for applicants and clubs to consult with responsible authorities when schedules are being prepared. This would allow for proper liaison before representations prove necessary.

CONSISTENCY WITH STEPS DESCRIBED IN OPERATING SCHEDULE

10.9 The 2003 Act provides that where an operating schedule or club operating schedule has been submitted with an application and there have been no relevant representations made by responsible authorities or interested parties, the licence or certificate must be granted subject only to such conditions as are consistent with the schedule accompanying the application and any mandatory conditions required by the Act itself.

Guidance issued under section 182 of the Licensing Act 2003

10.10 Consistency means that the effect of the condition should be substantially the same as that intended by the terms of the operating schedule or club operating schedule. Some applicants for licences or certificates supported by legal representatives or trade associations can be expected to express steps necessary to promote the licensing objectives in clear and readily translatable terms. However, some applicants will express the terms of their operating schedules less precisely or concisely. Ensuring that conditions are consistent with the operating schedule will then be more difficult. If conditions are broken this may lead to a criminal prosecution or an application for a review and it is extremely important therefore that they should be expressed on the licence or certificate in unequivocal and unambiguous terms. It must be clear to the holder of the licence or club, to enforcement officers and to the courts what duty has been placed on the holder or club in terms of compliance.

IMPOSED CONDITIONS

10.11 The licensing authority may not impose any conditions unless its discretion has been engaged following receipt of relevant representations and it has been satisfied at a hearing of the necessity to impose conditions. It may then only impose conditions that are necessary to promote one or more of the four licensing objectives. Such conditions must also be expressed in unequivocal and unambiguous terms to avoid legal dispute.

10.12 It is perfectly possible that in certain cases, because the test is one of necessity, where there are other legislative provisions which are relevant and must be observed by the applicant, no additional conditions at all are needed to promote the licensing objectives.

Proportionality

10.13 The Act requires that licensing conditions should be tailored to the size, style, characteristics and activities taking place at the premises concerned. This rules out standardised conditions which ignore these individual aspects. It is important that conditions are proportionate and properly recognise significant differences between venues. For example, charities, community groups, voluntary groups, churches, schools and hospitals which host smaller events and festivals will not usually be pursuing these events commercially with a view to profit and will inevitably operate within limited resources.

10.14 While the Secretary of State has set fees centrally for licences and certificates, licensing authorities and responsible authorities should be alive to the indirect costs that can arise because of conditions attached to licences. These could be a deterrent to holding events that are valuable to the community or for the funding of good and important causes. Such bodies may be loath to pursue appeals against any unnecessary conditions because of the costs involved. Licensing authorities should therefore ensure that any conditions they impose are only those which are necessary for the promotion of the licensing objectives, which means that they must not go further than what is needed for that purpose. Public safety concerns (and the concerns identified in the other objectives) should not of course be ignored and in considering a proportionate response to the licensing needs for such events, the physical safety of those attending such events should remain a primary objective.

Duplication with other statutory provisions

10.15 Licensing authorities should only impose conditions which are necessary and proportionate for the promotion for the licensing objectives. If other existing law already places certain statutory responsibilities on an employer or operator of premises, it cannot be necessary to impose the same or similar duties. For example, employers and self-employed people are required by the Management of Health and Safety at Work Regulations 1999 (SI 1999/3242) to assess the risks to their workers and any others (including members of the public visiting the premises) who may be affected by their business and identify measures needed to avoid or control risks. Conditions enforcing these requirements are therefore unnecessary.

10.16 Similarly, licensing authorities should not seek to impose fire safety conditions that may duplicate any requirements or prohibitions that could be imposed under the Regulatory Reform (Fire Safety) Order 2005 (see paragraphs 2.20 – 2.29).

10.17 Further, the Act does not affect the continued use of inspection and enforcement powers conferred by other legislation; for example, the powers of an environmental health officer in relation to statutory nuisance under the Environmental Protection Act 1990.

10.18 However, these general duties will not always adequately address specific issues that arise on the premises in connection with, for example, certain types of entertainment. It is only where additional and supplementary measures are necessary to promote the licensing objectives that conditions will need to be attached to a licence.

Hours of trading

10.19 In some town and city centre areas where the number, type and density of premises selling alcohol for consumption on the premises are unusual, serious problems of nuisance and disorder may arise outside or some distance from licensed premises. For example, concentrations of young drinkers can result in queues at fast food outlets and for public transport, which may in turn lead to conflict, disorder and anti-social behaviour. In some circumstances, flexible licensing hours may reduce this impact by allowing a more gradual dispersal of customers from premises.

10.20 However, there is no general presumption in favour of lengthening licensing hours and the four licensing objectives should be paramount considerations at all times. Where there are objections to an application and the committee believes that changing the licensing hours would undermine the licensing objectives, they may reject the application or grant it with appropriate conditions and/or different hours from those requested.

10.21 Shops, stores and supermarkets should normally be free to provide sales of alcohol for consumption off the premises at any times when the retail outlet is open for shopping unless there are good reasons, based on the licensing objectives, for restricting those hours. For example, a limitation may be appropriate following police representations in the case of some shops known to be a focus of disorder and disturbance because youths gather there.

Workers rights

10.22 It is not for the licensing authority to consider such matters as the rights of the workers employed on the premises who may be asked to work longer hours. There are existing protections under the Working Time Regulations 1998 (SI 1998/1833), the Employment Rights Act 1996 (as amended) and under the general employment law and laws of contract.

Disabled people

10.23 It is important that proper steps should be taken to provide for the safety of people and performers with disabilities. However, licensing authorities and responsible authorities should avoid well meaning conditions which are intended to provide for the safety of people or performers with disabilities, but which may actively deter operators from admitting or employing them.

10.24 It is Government policy that facilities for people and performers with disabilities should be provided at places of entertainment. The Secretary of State encourages licence holders and clubs to provide facilities enabling their admission and reminds them of the duties imposed by the Disability Discrimination Act 1995. The law provides that any person providing a service to the public must make reasonable adjustments to enable disabled people to access the service. No licensing condition should therefore be attached to a licence or certificate which conflicts with or duplicates this requirement.

10.25 Service providers also have a duty to make reasonable adjustments to any physical features which make it impossible or unreasonably difficult for disabled persons to access a service, or they have to provide the service by a reasonable alternative means. Access to buildings and their facilities is also a matter addressed in Building Regulations and planned alterations affecting access may involve the need to apply for building control.

10.26 Licensing authorities should therefore be ready to offer advice to applicants for licences and certificates about how to achieve this. Conditions which state that "wheelchairs and similar equipment shall not be allowed on the premises except in accordance with the terms of any consent issued by the licensing authority" can be ambiguous and be used to justify exclusion and may be ultra vires. Conditions should be positively worded and assume the presence of people with disabilities on licensed premises.

10.27 In addition, Government guidelines exempting guide and assistance dogs from health and safety requirements have been in place since 1995. Any condition of a licence or certificate which states that "pets" may not be present on licensed premises for public safety reasons, must include a clear indication that the condition does not apply to guide or assistance dogs. Further advice can be obtained from the Disability Rights Commission's website www.drc-gb.org.

10.28 The Disability Discrimination Act 1995 does not apply to ships. However the European Council Directive 2003/24/EC requires appropriate measures to be taken for 'persons of reduced mobility' (this means anyone who has a particular difficulty when using public transport; including elderly persons, disabled persons, persons with sensory impairments and wheelchair users, pregnant women and persons accompanying small children) on certain passenger ships engaged on domestic voyages. Further advice and guidance is contained in Merchant Shipping Notice 1789 (M) and Marine Guidance Note 306 (M) both of which are available in the Guidance and Regulations section of the Maritime and Coastguard Agency's website www.mcga.gov.uk. These documents complement the existing guidance 'The design of large passenger ships and passenger infrastructure: Guidance on meeting the needs of disabled people' which is available on the website of the Disabled Persons Transport Advisory Committee at www.dptac.gov.uk in the maritime section.

Race equality

10.29 Licensing authorities should also avoid imposing any condition on a licence or certificate which appears to apply to a wide group of people, but in fact would have an indirect discriminatory impact on particular ethnic groups. For example, a representation requesting that "No Travellers" or "No Caravan-Dwellers" be displayed inside or on premises purportedly to prevent crime or disorder should not be accepted not least because it would conflict with the authority's race equality scheme.

The performance of plays

10.30 The 2003 Act provides that other than for the purposes of public safety, conditions must not be attached to premises licences or club premises certificates authorising the performance of a play which attempt to censor or modify the content of plays in any way. Any such condition would be ultra vires the Act.

Censorship

10.31 In general, other than in the context of film classification for film exhibitions, licensing authorities should not use their powers under the 2003 Act to seek to impose conditions which censor the content of any form of regulated entertainment. This is not a proper function of licensing law and cannot be properly related to the licensing objectives. The content of regulated entertainment is a matter which is addressed by existing laws governing indecency and obscenity. Where the concern is about protecting children, their access should be restricted where necessary. But no other limitation should normally be imposed.

Guidance issued under section 182 of the Licensing Act 2003

Copyright and royalties

10.32 Copyright law is intended to safeguard the livelihood of authors, composers, arrangers, playwrights, film-makers, publishers and makers of recordings and is extremely important and offences relating to copyright are made "relevant offences" by the 2003 Act. Conditions attached to premises licences should not require adherence to requirements in the general law that the use of copyright material must be authorised. Licensing authorities should however strongly remind applicants of the need to obtain Performing Right Society (PRS) licences and Phonographic Performance Ltd (PPL) licences and to observe other copyright arrangements; and that failure to observe the law in this area could lead to an application for the review of the premises licence or the club premises certificate on grounds of the crime prevention objective.

Major art and pop festivals, carnivals, fairs and circuses

10.33 Licensing authorities should publicise the need for the organisers of major festivals and carnivals to approach them at the earliest opportunity to discuss arrangements for licensing activities falling under the 2003 Act. For some events, the organisers may seek a single premises licence to cover a wide range of activities at varied locations within the premises. This would involve the preparation of a substantial operating schedule, and licensing authorities should offer advice and assistance about its preparation. In particular, the licensing authority should act as a co-ordinating body for the input from the responsible authorities.

10.34 For other events, applications for many connected premises licences may be made which in combination will represent a single festival. It is important that licensing authorities should publicise the need for proper co-ordination of such arrangements and will need to ensure that responsible authorities are aware of the connected nature of the individual applications. Licensing authorities should encourage applicants to establish a co-ordinating committee to ensure a strategic approach to the development of operating schedules. The purpose would be to ensure that conditions are not included in licences which conflict with each other, make compliance uncertain or would be difficult to enforce.

10.35 In the case of circuses and fairgrounds, much will depend on the content of any entertainment presented. For example, at fairgrounds, a good deal of the musical entertainment may be incidental to the main attractions and rides at the fair which are not themselves regulated entertainment. However, in the case of a circus, music and dancing are likely to be main attractions themselves (and would be regulated entertainment) amidst a range of other activities which are not all regulated entertainment.

10.36 Particular regard should be paid to the relevant guidance provided in the publications listed at Annex E of this Guidance under 'Public Safety'.

10.37 In addition, in the context of festivals and carnivals, local authorities should bear in mind their ability to seek premises licences from the licensing authority for land or buildings under public ownership within the community in their own name. This could include, for example, village greens, market squares, promenades, community halls, local authority owned art centres and similar public areas where festivals and carnivals might take place. Performers and entertainers would then have no need to obtain a licence or give a temporary event notice themselves to enable them to give performances in these places, although they would need the permission of the local authority to put on the event. Care should be exercised to ensure that there is no confusion between the role of enforcing licensing legislation, which falls to the licensing authority, and the role of providing advice and assistance to festival and carnival organisers from other parts of the local authority.

Fixed prices

10.38 Licensing authorities should not attach standardised blanket conditions promoting fixed prices for alcoholic drinks to premises licences or club licences or club premises certificates in an area as this is likely to breach competition law. It is also likely to be unlawful for licensing authorities or the police to promote generalised voluntary schemes or codes of practice in relation to price discounts on alcoholic drinks, 'happy hours' or drinks promotions. However, it is important to note that the mandatory conditions made under section 19A of the 2003 Act prohibit a number of types of drinks promotions where they give rise to a significant risk of not promoting any one of the four licensing objectives. The Government recommends that licensing authorities, police, trading standards, local trade and other partners should discuss and reach agreement as to how those mandatory conditions translate to actual promotions in the local area and, ideally, reach a common shared understanding of what types of promotion are likely to be considered irresponsible. Please refer to the Home Office Guidance on the mandatory conditions for further information (http://www.homeoffice.gov.uk/crime-victims/reducing-crime/alcohol-related-crime/).

10.39 Where licensing authorities are asked by the police, other responsible authorities or interested parties to impose restrictions on promotions in addition to those restricted by the mandatory conditions, they should consider each application on its individual merits, tailoring any conditions carefully to cover only irresponsible promotions in the particular and individual circumstances of any premises where these are necessary for the promotion of the licensing objectives. In addition, when considering any relevant representations which demonstrate a clear causal link between sales promotions or price discounting and levels of crime and disorder on or in the vicinity of the premises, it would be appropriate for the licensing authority to consider the imposition of a new condition prohibiting irresponsible sales promotions or the discounting of prices of alcoholic beverages at those premises. However, before pursuing any form of restrictions at all, licensing authorities should take their own legal advice. There will often be very fine lines between what is and is not lawful within the scope of their power under the 2003 Act.

Guidance issued under section 182 of the Licensing Act 2003

Large capacity venues used exclusively or primarily for the "vertical" consumption of alcohol (HVVDs)

10.40 Large capacity "vertical drinking" premises, sometimes called High Volume Vertical Drinking establishments (HVVDs), are premises with exceptionally high capacities, which are used primarily or exclusively for the sale and consumption of alcohol, and have little or no seating for patrons.

10.41 A comprehensive review of the research conducted in the last twenty-five years into alcohol and crime and its relationship to licensed premises, "Alcohol and Crime: Taking Stock" by Ann Deehan, Home Office Crime Reduction Research Series No.3 (1999) can be viewed on www.crimereduction.gov.uk/drugsalcohol8.htm. It shows that the environment within such establishments can have a significant bearing on the likelihood of crime and disorder arising on the premises. Key points on preventing crime and disorder include:

- controlling the capacity to prevent overcrowding and frustration to customers;
- ensuring adequate seating for customers; and
- ensuring the provision of door security teams at the premises to control capacity and ensure already drunk or disorderly individuals are not admitted.

10.42 Where necessary and appropriate, conditions can be attached to premises licences for the promotion of the prevention of crime and disorder at such premises (if not volunteered by the venue operator and following representations made on such grounds) which require adherence to:

- a prescribed capacity;
- an appropriate ratio of tables and chairs to customers based on the capacity; and
- the presence of security staff holding the appropriate SIA licence or exemption (see paragraphs 10.58-10.64) to control entry for the purpose of compliance with the capacity limit and to deny entry to individuals who appear drunk or disorderly or both.

MANDATORY CONDITIONS

10.43 The 2003 Act provides for the following mandatory conditions to be included in every licence and/or club premises certificate.

Mandatory conditions in relation to the supply of alcohol

Designated Premises Supervisor

10.44 Any premises at which alcohol is sold or supplied may employ one or more personal licence holders. The main purpose of the 'designated premises supervisor' as defined in the 2003 Act is to ensure that there is always one specified individual among these personal licence holders who can be readily identified for the premises where a premises licence is in force. That person will normally have been given day to day responsibility for running the premises by the premises licence holder. The requirements set out in paragraph 10.46 to 10.53 below in relation to the designated premises supervisor and authorisation of alcohol sales by a personal licence holder do not apply to community premises in respect of which a successful application has been made to disapply the usual mandatory conditions in sections 19(2) and 19(3) of the 2003 Act (see paragraphs 4.32 to 4.47 of this Guidance).

10.45 The 2003 Act provides that, where a premises licence authorises the supply of alcohol, it must include a condition that no supply of alcohol may be made at a time when no designated premises supervisor has been specified in the licence or at a time when the designated premises supervisor does not hold a personal licence or their licence has been suspended.

10.46 The Act does not require a designated premises supervisor or any other personal licence holder to be present on the premises at all times when alcohol is sold. However, the designated premises supervisor and the premises licence holder remain responsible for the premises at all times including compliance with the terms of the Licensing Act and conditions attached to the premises licence to promote the licensing objectives.

Authorisation by personal licence holders

10.47 In addition, the licence must require that every supply of alcohol under the premises licence must be made or authorised by a person who holds a personal licence. This in most instances will be the designated premises supervisor who must hold a valid personal licence. This does not mean that the condition should require the presence of the designated premises supervisor or any other personal licence holder on the premises at all material times.

10.48 Similarly, the fact that every supply of alcohol must be made under the authority of a personal licence holder does not mean that only personal licence holders can make sales or that they must be personally present at every transaction. A personal licence holder may authorise members of staff to make sales of alcohol but may be absent at times from the premises when a transaction takes place. However, the responsible personal licence holder will not be able to escape responsibility for the actions of anyone authorised to make sales.

10.49 "Authorisation" does not imply direct supervision by a personal licence holder of each sale of alcohol. The question arises as to how sales can be authorised. Ultimately, whether an authorisation has been given is a question of fact that would have to be decided by the courts on the evidence before it in the course of a criminal prosecution.

10.50 Nevertheless, it is important that licensing authorities, the police, employers and employees in the alcohol retail industry are given advice which promotes greater clarity and consistency. The Secretary of State considers that the following factors should be relevant in considering whether or not an authorisation has been given:

- the person(s) authorised to sell alcohol at any particular premises should be clearly identified;
- the authorisation should have specified the acts which may be carried out by the person being authorised;
- there should be an overt act of authorisation, for example, a specific written statement given to the individual being authorised; and
- there should be in place sensible arrangements for the personal licence holder to monitor the activity that they have authorised on a reasonably regular basis.

10.51 The Secretary of State strongly recommends that personal licence holders give specific written authorisations to individuals that they are authorising to retail alcohol. A single written authorisation would be sufficient to cover multiple sales over an unlimited period. This would assist personal licence holders in demonstrating due diligence should issues arise with enforcement authorities; and would protect employees if they themselves are challenged in respect of their authority to sell alcohol. The form of written authorisation is a matter for the personal licence holder, but the Secretary of State recommends that it should satisfy the criteria listed in the paragraph above. Written authorisation is not a requirement of the Act and its absence alone could not give rise to enforcement action.

10.52 It must be remembered that whilst the designated premises supervisor or a personal licence holder may authorise other individuals to sell alcohol in their absence, they are responsible for any sales that may be made. Similarly, the premises licence holder remains responsible for ensuring that licensing law and licence conditions are observed at the premises, and is also responsible for alcohol sales at community premises where the usual mandatory conditions in sections 19(2) and 19(3) of the 2003 Act relating to personal licence holders and Designated Premises Supervisors have been disapplied (see paragraphs 4.32 to 4.47 of this Guidance).

Arrangements for the new mandatory conditions

10.53 The new mandatory conditions introduced in section 19A of the 2003 Act (governing e.g. irresponsible promotions), unlike the existing mandatory conditions (e.g. the requirement for a Designated Premises Supervisor under section 19 of the 2003 Act), do not have to be physically included in the licence or certificate but nonetheless will apply to every licence and certificate authorising the sale and supply of alcohol for consumption on the premises. However, like the existing mandatory conditions, the new mandatory conditions do not apply to activities (including the supply of alcohol) authorised by a temporary event notice.

10.54 Whereas the existing mandatory conditions are set out in Annex A of the licence or certificate, the new mandatory conditions are treated as if they were included in existing licences and certificates on the date that they came into force.

10.55 The new mandatory conditions override any pre-existing conditions already included in a licence or certificate insofar as the new mandatory conditions are identical to, or inconsistent with and more onerous than, any pre-existing conditions. The new mandatory conditions take effect on this basis in relation to existing licences and certificates on the date that the new mandatory conditions come into force, and the impact this will have on pre-existing conditions written into existing licences and certificates will not be recorded on the face of those documents. Local Authorities may like to make licence and certificate holders aware that the new conditions apply, to enable them to check that they thereafter operate in accordance with any changes which have been made to their conditions. Licensing Authorities may also wish to make license holders aware of Home Office Guidance on the new mandatory conditions (see 10.38 for weblink).

Irresponsible promotions

10.56 Under this condition, the "responsible person" (defined in the 2003 Act as the holder of a premises licence, designated premises supervisor, a person aged 18 or over who is authorised to allow the sale or supply of alcohol by an under 18 or a member or officer of a club present on the club premises who can oversee the supply of alcohol) should be able to demonstrate that they have taken all reasonable steps to ensure that staff do not carry out, arrange or participate in any irresponsible promotions. An irresponsible promotion is one which encourages the sale or supply of alcohol for consumption on the premises and carries a significant risk of leading or contributing to crime and disorder, prejudice to public safety, public nuisance or harm to children. The aim of the condition is to prohibit or restrict promotions which encourage people to drink more than they might ordinarily do and in a manner which does not promote the licensing objectives.

10.57 Irresponsible promotions take a number of forms. The following activities are set out under the 2003 Act and cover the specific activities described below or those that are substantially similar. Please refer to guidance issued by the Home Office for fuller understanding of irresponsible promotions (see 10.38 for weblink).

Drinking Games

10.58 Drinking games are those which may require or encourage individuals to drink a quantity of alcohol within a time limit, or drink as much alcohol as possible within a time limit or otherwise. For example, this may include organised 'drink downing' competitions if these carry a significant risk to any of the four licensing objectives. This would not prevent the responsible person (see paragraph 10.56) from requiring all drinks to be consumed or abandoned at, or before, the closing time of the premises. Nor does it necessarily prohibit 'happy hours' as long as these are not designed to encourage individuals to drink excessively or rapidly.

Large Quantities of Alcohol For Free or A Fixed Price

10.59 The sale, supply or provision of unlimited or unspecified quantities of alcohol free or for a fixed or discounted price to the public or to a group defined by a particular characteristic. This does not apply to a promotion or discount on alcohol for consumption with a table meal. However, it may apply specifically to promotions aimed at groups that are defined by a particular characteristic if there is a significant risk that this does not promote the licensing objectives. This restriction does not mean that promotions cannot be designed with a particular group in mind but a common sense approach is encouraged, for example, by specifying the quantity of alcohol included in the promotion and not targeting groups that may become more vulnerable, or present a greater risk of crime and disorder, as a result of excessive alcohol consumption. For example, this prohibition is likely to apply to deals such as "all you can drink for £10".

Prizes and Rewards

10.60 The sale, supply or provision of free or discounted alcohol or any other item as a prize to encourage or reward the purchase and consumption of alcohol over a period of 24 hours or less where there is a significant risk to any of the four licensing objectives.

Sporting Events

10.61 The sale, supply or provision of alcohol for free or for a discounted price in relation to a sporting event shown on the premises, where the sale etc. depends on the outcome of a race, match or other event. For example, this may include offering unlimited drinks based on the outcome of a sporting competition where there is a significant risk to any of the four licensing objectives. It also applies to events which are unpredictable, such as offering free double shots for every foul committed in a football match, or heavily reduced drinks for five minutes after a try is scored in a rugby match.

Posters and Flyers

10.62 The sale or supply of alcohol in association with promotional materials on display in or around the premises, which can either be reasonably considered to condone, encourage or glamorise anti social behaviour or refer to the effects of drunkenness in any favourable manner.

Dispensing alcohol directly into the mouth

10.63 The responsible person (see paragraph 10.56) must ensure that no alcohol is dispensed directly by one person into the mouth of another person. For example, this may include drinking games such as the 'dentist's chair' where a drink is poured continuously into the mouth of another individual and may also prevent a premises from allowing another body to promote its products by employing someone to dispense alcohol directly into customers' mouths. An exception to this condition would be when an individual is unable to drink without assistance due to a disability.

Free tap water

10.64 The responsible person (see paragraph 10.56) must ensure that free potable tap water is provided on request to customers where it is reasonably available on the premises. What is meant by reasonably available is a question of fact; for example, it would not be reasonable to expect free tap water to be available in premises for which the water supply had temporarily been lost because of a broken mains water supply.

Age-verification

10.65 The premises licence holder or club premises certificate holder must ensure that an age verification policy applies to the premises in relation to the sale or supply of alcohol. This must as a minimum require individuals who appear to the responsible person (see paragraph 10.56) to be under the age of 18 years of age to produce on request, before being served alcohol, identification bearing their photograph, date of birth, and a holographic mark.

10.66 It should be noted that it is acceptable, and indeed encouraged, for premises to have an age verification policy which requires individuals who appear to the responsible person to be under an age greater than 18 to produce such identification on request. For example, if a premises has a policy that

requires any individual that appears to be under the age of 21 to produce identification that meets the criteria listed above, this is perfectly acceptable under the mandatory code.

10.67 The age-verification condition ordinarily only applies in situations where the sale takes place face to face. Companies that sell alcohol remotely (e.g. online or by mail order) should operate an age verification policy, but as the sale of alcohol does not ordinarily take place on delivery, the condition does not in such cases require photo ID to be shown at the point of delivery. As long as age verification has taken place already via another means, these transactions will meet the requirement of the condition.

10.68 The premises licence holder or club premises certificate holder must ensure that staff (in particular staff who are involved in the supply of alcohol) are made aware of the existence and content of the age verification policy applied by the premises.

Smaller Measures

10.69 The responsible person (see paragraph 10.56) shall ensure that the following drinks if sold or supplied on the premises are available in the following measures:

· Beer or cider – 1/2 pint
· Gin, rum, vodka or whisky – 25ml or 35ml
· Still wine in a glass: 125ml

10.70 As well as making the drinks available in the above measures, the responsible person must also make customers aware of the availability of these measures – for example, by making their availability clear on menus and price lists, and ensuring that these are displayed in a prominent place in the relevant premises (e.g. at the bar).

Guidance issued under section 182 of the Licensing Act 2003

10.71 The above condition does not apply if the drinks in question are sold or supplied having been made up in advance ready for sale or supply in a securely closed container. For example, if beer is only available in pre-sealed bottles the condition to make it available in 1/2 pints does not apply.

10.72 The premises licence holder or club premises certificate holder must ensure that staff are made aware of the application of this condition.

Exhibition of films

10.73 The 2003 Act provides that where a premises licence or club premises certificate authorises the exhibition of a film, it must include a condition requiring the admission of children to films to be restricted in accordance with recommendations given either by a body designated under section 4 of the Video Recordings Act 1984 specified in the licence (currently only the British Board of Film Classification – BBFC) or by the licensing authority itself.

10.74 The BBFC classifies films in accordance with its published Guidelines which are based on extensive research into public opinion and professional advice. The Secretary of State therefore recommends that licensing authorities should not duplicate this effort by choosing to classify films themselves. The classifications recommended by the Board should be those normally applied unless there are very good local reasons for a licensing authority to adopt this role. Licensing authorities should note that the provisions of the 2003 Act enable them to specify the Board in the licence or certificate and, in relation to individual films, to notify the holder or club that it will make a recommendation for that particular film.

10.75 It should be noted that the effect of paragraph 5 of Schedule 1 of the Act is to exempt adverts from the definition of regulated entertainment, but not to exempt them from the definition of exhibition of a film. Since the above mandatory condition applies to 'any film' it is therefore applicable to the exhibition of adverts.

10.76 See Annex D, Part 5 for further Guidance on current BBFC classifications and other conditions relating to the exhibition of films.

Door supervision

10.77 Under section 21 of the 2003 Act when a condition is included in a premises licence that at specified times an individual must be present at the premises to carry out a security activity (as defined in section 21(3)(a) by reference to the Private Security Industry Act 2001 ("the 2001 Act")), the licence must include a condition requiring that individual to be licensed by the Security Industry Authority ("the SIA") under that Act, or be entitled to carry out that activity by virtue of section 4 of that Act.

10.78 Section 21 of the 2003 Act has been amended by section 25 of the Violent Crime Reduction Act 2006 to remove an anomaly whereby premises licences could require persons to be licensed by the SIA in circumstances where they were not required to be licensed under the 2001 Act. In particular, the amendment ensures that a premises licence need not require a person to hold a Security Industry Authority licence if they benefit from an exemption under section 4 of the 2001 Act. By way of example, certain employees benefit from an exemption when carrying out conduct in connection with a certified sports grounds (s.4(6 to 12)). Furthermore, in certain circumstances persons benefit from an exemption where they operate under the SIA's Approved Contractor Scheme (s4(4)).

10.79 Conditions under section 21 of the 2003 Act (as amended by the Violent Crime Reduction Act 2006) should only relate to individuals carrying out security activities defined by section 21(3)(a) of the 2003 Act. Therefore they should only relate to an activity to which paragraph 2(1)(a) of Schedule 2 to the 2001 Act applies (certain manned guarding activities) and which is licensable conduct within the meaning of section 3(2) of that Act. The requirement does not relate to individuals performing non-security related activities, and section 21 should not be used in relation to any such activities.

10.80 Section 21 of the 2003 Act continues to ensure that a premises licence need not impose such a requirement in relation to those licensed premises which the 2001 Act treats as unlicensed premises. Those are:

- premises staging plays or exhibiting films;
- casinos or bingo halls licensed under the Gaming Act 1968;
- premises where a club certificate is in force when activities are being carried on under the authority of that certificate;

See paragraph 8(3) of Schedule 2 to the 2001 Act for full details.

10.81 It should be noted, however, that the 2001 Act will require contractors and a small number of employees (those managing/supervising and those supplied under contract) to be licensed as manned guards (rather than door supervisors) when undertaking licensable conduct on premises to which paragraph 8(3) of Schedule 2 to the 2001 Act applies.

10.82 It is therefore important that if a licensing authority intends that individuals must be present to carry out security activities (as defined by section 21(3)(a) of the 2003 Act) this should be explicit, as should the mandatory condition for those individuals to hold an SIA licence or be entitled to carry out that activity by virtue of section 4 of that Act. On the other hand, where a licensing authority intends that individuals must be present to carry out other activities (for example, activities related to safety or steward activities to organise, advise and direct members of the public) no mandatory condition should be imposed under section 21 of the 2003 Act. In all cases it is important when determining whether or not a condition is to be imposed under section 21 of the 2003 Act to consider whether the activities of any individual working in licensed premises fall within the definition of security activities in section 21(3)(a) of the 2003 Act. (Regardless of whether a condition is imposed under section 21, under the 2001 Act the appropriate SIA licence must be held by any individual performing an activity for which they are licensable under that Act).

10.83 Holders of premises licences should note that the amendment under the Violent Crime Reduction Act 2006 will not affect the requirements in existing licences regarding security provision. Anyone wishing to deploy staff under the terms of the amended legislation and whose licence does not permit them to do so will need to apply to have their licence varied. The Government recommends that where an application is made to vary a licence solely in order to remove the anomaly referred to in paragraph 10.59 the licensing authority should treat the matter as expeditiously as possible, in recognition of the fact that the variation sought will almost always be purely technical in nature.

Index

References are to page numbers